AW WITH WORDS

Young Writers' 16th Annual Poetry Competition

It is feeling and force of imagination that make us eloquent.

How can I not dream while writing? The blank page gives a right to dream.

YoungWriters

Merseyside

Edited by Heather Killingray

Young Writers
First published in Great Britain in 2007 by:
Young Writers
Remus House
Coltsfoot Drive
Peterborough
PE2 9JX
Telephone: 01733 890066
Website: www.youngwriters.co.uk

SB ISBN 978-1 84431 108 8

Foreword

This year, the Young Writers' *Away With Words* competition proudly presents a showcase of the best poetic talent selected from thousands of up-and-coming writers nationwide.

Young Writers was established in 1991 to promote the reading and writing of poetry within schools and to the young of today. Our books nurture and inspire confidence in the ability of young writers and provide a snapshot of poems written in schools and at home by budding poets of the future.

The thought, effort, imagination and hard work put into each poem impressed us all and the task of selecting poems was a difficult but nevertheless enjoyable experience.

We hope you are as pleased as we are with the final selection and that you and your family continue to be entertained with *Away With Words Merseyside* for many years to come.

Contents

St Augustine of Canterbury Catholic High School, St Helens

The Poems

Polar Bear, Polar Bear

Polar bear, polar bear, white as snow
Polar bear, polar bear, I expect you to be slow
Polar bear, polar bear, you move so fast
Polar bear, polar bear, your home won't last.

You glide through the water, looking for prey
You crawl on land, beaten by a walrus, where you lay
Your poor bloodstained back
With the blood that you suffered from your walrus attack.

Polar bear, polar bear, white as snow
Polar bear, polar bear, I expect you to be slow
Polar bear, polar bear, you move so fast
Polar bear, polar bear, your home won't last.

Jake Barton (12)
Birkdale High School

Heart Of The Mountain

In the heart of a mountain,
A dragon lies spitting lava like a fountain.
Many noble knights have tried to slay,
Our dragon who keeps them all locked away.

Bones have been scattered around,
The last time a knight was found.
A brave knight enters the mountain,
Seeing a lava-spewing fountain.

Knowing that the dragon is near,
He suddenly feels a surge of fear.
He tries to tread as lightly as he can,
But the dragon knows there is a man,
Lurking in his banished domain.
He searches, but then feels a piercing pain.

The sword is driven into the dragon's toe,
The knight knowing he has made a menacing foe.
The dragon relishing a menacing wrath,
The knight sprinting down an empty path.

The dragon picking up the pace,
Fire coming from its cavernous face.
The knight feels the terror,
But has made a crucial error.

Running into a dead end,
The dragon's tail coming round the bend.
The dragon eyes his prey,
The knight's life ending in horror and dismay.

Ryan Hale (12)
Birkdale High School

Cheesy Pie

On a plate sit two cheese pies
Staring at me like a pair of eyes
Not too long and they will be in my belly
Sloshing around like a big bowl of jelly.

The soothing aroma, wafting around my nose
The cheesy goodness, o' how it glows
I'm going to tuck in now, leave me alone,
If I was denied this delicacy, I would certainly groan.

Rory Boyer (13)
Birkdale High School

Who Are You?

I woke up one day,
In a strange bed I lay,
Didn't recognise it,
The room vaguely lit.

The mirror looked at me,
I didn't know what I saw,
Knock, knock! What would it be,
People at the front door?

I opened it slightly,
And asked them politely,
'Who are you?'
They replied, 'Do you need a clue?'

Thinking I was being funny,
They walked in and then sat down,
Halfway through asking for money,
One stopped when he noticed my frown.

I told them I was serious,
Confused and bewildered, they said,
'We are your best mates, yes, that's us,'
Nervously spoken, 'What's going through my head?'

They told me of things I had done,
My friends and family and my past,
They showed me trophies that I had won,
Finally, took me to memories last.

After a while I remembered some things
And gradually got used to my life.
I visited a psychiatrist, who was wearing rings,
She told me that she was my wife.

It turns out amnesia has changed me,
I don't even remember who I am you see!

Rachel Chadwick (12)
Birkenhead High School

Why I Am Nervous?

I opened my eyes
I saw the birds fly by
I thought to myself
I'm getting married today
Why am I nervous?
I love the one I'm about to marry
So why, oh why, am I nervous?
I heard my bedroom door open
My mum standing there with breakfast
I wasn't hungry
Time passed by
It was time to put on my dress
Why, oh why am I still nervous?
Smiling for all the pictures
Bridesmaids looking beautiful
Time to go to church
Looking out the window
As we approach the church
People standing watching me
Why, oh why, am I still nervous?
Getting out of the car
Gasps of excitement around me
Thinking to myself
Why, oh why, am I still nervous?
Standing in the entrance of the church
Ready to go
The sound of the organ playing
My dream came true.

Georgie Betts (12)
Birkenhead High School

Dreams

When you close your eyes in bed,
When the day is over and dead,
You've read your book and counted the sheep
You're drowsy and you want to sleep
So you lay on your side and rest your head
And think of the day that lies ahead.

Wait! Shush! You tell your thoughts
The light has stopped shining from under your door
Someone is tired and going to sleep,
'They're lucky,' you sigh as they quietly creep
Their footsteps are light on the carpeted floor,
They close their eyes as you softly snore.

You feel on your face a backwards frown,
As you find that gravity doesn't pull you back down
To Earth - no not Earth - you smile as you see
But a dreamland as beautiful as can be.
What a wonderful world, you sigh and look around
As you float away on a fluffy white cloud.

And just when you think that no sorrow can come
You hear a voice in your head, and a voice starts to hum
The most hated song that you have ever known
As you realise what it is, you let out a groan
You recognise the tune and happy melody,
It is the sound of your alarm clock, it taunts you, can it be?

The blue sky around you turns to a dark abyss
You sigh as you feel your dream's last kiss,
You have no choice, so you jump into the hole
That surrounds you, you're falling as the bell tolls
On your dreams you stretch out your fingers and are surprised
To find yourself in your bed, so you open your eyes.

Kaedy Bryson (13)
Birkenhead High School

Neglected Dog

I wake to find my owner eating breakfast
The smell of bacon is in the air
I sit in my small cardboard box
Staring at my bowl which is empty and bare.

I wait for a walk which never comes
My fur hasn't been washed, it's awfully smelly
I have to eat something, I think I could die
I look around and choose my owner's welly.

Pain shoots through my ribs
I'm so weak I scramble to my bed
I hate my owner
I wish she was dead.

A woman came to take me away
I was confused and didn't know why
She looked very friendly and treated me well
I looked back, my owner let out a huge sigh.

I play with dogs every hour
And get a long walk every day
My new owner is very friendly
Now all I do is play.

Lucy Green (12)
Birkenhead High School

When I Was Young . . .

When I was young,
I wished to be on The Tweenies,
Milo, Jake, Fizz and Bella,
They are all best friends together,
Messy time and story time,
Reading books and writing rhymes.

When I was young,
I wished to be on Balamory,
Archie, Spencer and PC Plum,
Every scene was set in the sun,
Josie, Suzie and Miss Hoolie too,
They have so much fun with me and you.

When I was young,
I wished to be on Big Cook, Little Cook,
In their kitchen they had so much fun,
Making their own pink iced buns,
I loved to watch them cook,
I thought it was better than reading a book.

When I was young,
I wished to be on Winnie the Pooh
Winnie, Piglet, Eeyore and Tigger,
They lived across from the 100 acre river,
Christopher Robin is Winnie's best friend,
I wish this poem would never end.

Rebecca Gibson (12)
Birkenhead High School

The Theory

I have a theory,
People argue all the time about who or what created the Earth.
God or science?

Well I have a theory,
It will amaze you, it will, it will put to rest the argument.
God or science?

This theory will change the way everyone thinks about
The Earth and life as we know it.
God or science?

People who have spent their lives arguing,
Minds will be put to rest.
God or science?

I have a theory
Here it is
It's all in the past.
We can't change it
We can't relive it
Why bother?
We have an amazing world with natural beauty
The rainforests
The vast oceans
Why dwell on the past
When you can dwell on the future?

Nicola Fletcher (13)
Birkenhead High School

A Mysterious Object

I am everywhere,
In all different sizes and shapes
I can look quite bare
But sometimes I am covered in tape.

I am in Spain
I am in France
I may cause you pain
I can be passed without a glance.

I am in The States
I am in Hong Kong
I am in the Tate
I am where you have a singsong.

I am in boats
I am in plays
I do tend to float
I am in a nice shop called Kays.

But there is one thing you must know
I don't move, I stand still all day
You use me to go
I cannot say.

Like I said, if you look you will find me
My life may sound a bore
Down my throat you stick a key
If you have guessed then well done because I am a door.

Lottie Elliott (12)
Birkenhead High School

The Earth

What is the Earth?
I think it is a place full of adventures,
An explorer's paradise,
People's homes.
A spotty green and blue ball.
A world packed with different tribes and animals,
A place bursting with buildings,
A world buzzing with technology,
A place filled with rainforests and cities,
Important people who change the world for good and bad.
Antartica, an ice world filled with animals and beauty.
Which is sadly being destroyed.
Beaches and palm trees that sway in the wind.
Animals and people living happy lives,
Fine buildings.
Sadly sometimes ferocious oceans.
This is the world,
It can stay this way
But it needs our help.

Emma Jones (12)
Birkenhead High School

Darkness

Whichever way I turn,
All I see is darkness,
As though I am in a cave,
Struggling to find a way out;
But I know I never will,
Because I am blind.

Each day I wake,
I still hear those odious words;
'You can never have your eyesight back.'
I regret what I did now in my past.

Night was falling,
But the celebration was just about to begin.
I stood there watching the bonfire flames dance around;
Though I did not notice they were creeping closer towards me,
Then when I did, it was too late.
I was trapped.

I can't remember what happened next,
But hearing that I was in a hospital;
I heard my story on the news
That was when I realised,
My life was destroyed.

So whichever way I turn,
All I see is darkness;
As though I am in a cave,
Struggling to find a way out;
But I know I never will
Because I am blind.

Rebecca Hughes (13)
Birkenhead High School

Losing Your Mum

Standing by the newly-made grave,
My heart bleeds with sorrow,
I close my eyes and wish,
Wish that it all never happened,
Wish that the car hadn't come.

She had created me,
Loved me the day I was born.
So why did she suffer that way?
Why? She was my best friend,
My carer and my favourite person in the world.

I loved her with my heart and soul,
Oh I miss my mummy so much,
But at least I know she's happy,
Perhaps resting on a cloud in Heaven
Watching my every step . . .

Natalie Ho (13)
Birkenhead High School

My Life Of Happiness!

I was bullied,
But now I find happiness
I now can find confidence.

I had told my parents
I am finding happiness
My life was full of misery
Now my life is full of joy.

I find it much easier to communicate
I felt that I was lost
But now I feel that I am found.

I have not all the joy
But most of my life is full of it!

My schoolwork was appalling
Now it is good!

I have a feeling of great happiness
I enjoy lots.

My real friends helped me
The bullies destroyed my happiness.

My life is much better
But at times, I feel sorry for those who are in the situation as me!

I wish I were able to support them all
But I am not.

What are bullies for?

Making lives miserable
Making people feel bad
Or is it both?

I am much happier now
But are you?

Petina Liu (12)
Birkenhead High School

Dreams

Dreams are wishes
Dreams are magical
Dreams are full of happiness
Dreams are full of love

Dreams can be fairy tales
Dreams can be horror stories
That frighten you
Shivering down your spine.

Happy dreams
That you want to keep
Sad dreams
That you want to die away.

Hold onto dreams
As when they're gone
They won't come back.

Susannah Knight (12)
Birkenhead High School

Out In The Sea . . .

It was windy, rainy and wild, out in the sea,
A fearless ship was fighting
Its way through the angry waves,
The wind howled and wailed.

As the weather worsened
The ship was losing its strength and courage,
Suddenly there was a loud noise,
And the ship was devoured by the angry waves.

Viveta Karunakaram (12)
Birkenhead High School

While I Drifted Away . . .

As I looked across the sea
The sun was sparkling on the calm water
It was a warm sunny day
The quilt of blue covering the bottom of the boat
The smell of the salty water in the air
The sound of the seagulls squawking
As I drifted way . . . I woke up
The wind was howling, blowing against my red cheeks
The waves crashing against the boat
The dark grey sky flashing lines of silver
Quicker than quick the rain heavily began to fall
The temperature dropped as it got worse and worse
The boat started to tip to one side making the water come aboard
The water is up to my knees, what will I do,
Just what am I going to do?
My tears blending in with the raindrops on my face
Please be a dream, please be a dream.

Sophia Nikolaou (12)
Birkenhead High School

The Netball Game

The whistle blows, a high-pitch shriek,
As the players run their trainers squeak.
Bodies dart, fast and furious,
Aiming to score triumphant and glorious,
The ball soars through the sky,
Players jumping and reaching up high.
The players fall hot and bothered,
To regain from their shame.
They shout at others to take the blame.
Now it gets competitive, charging and barging
Netball is quick and rough,
Some people may find it tough.

Leagha Naylor (13)
Birkenhead High School

The End

I sit still on the cold hard tarmac,
Rocking back and forth,
My sodden clothes cling to me,
While my brother lies dead and cold.

A stranger comes to approach me,
I simply widen my eyes and stare,
The crushed, mangled car lies behind me,
The killer had not a care.

The street lamp flickers above me,
And the fog floats further down,
My heart is swollen deep inside me,
My pain is hard to bear.

I close my eyes tight shut,
Wishing to be anywhere but here,
But the only thoughts I remember
Are hanging painfully in the air.

That white van is swerving again,
My screams are penetrating,
Echoing around,
The flicker of the headlights is blinding,
My brother struggles to avoid, but too late,
He's too late,
And here I am once again, swaying on this concrete bend,
The last moments I had with my brother are tragic,
His life is at its end.

Sarah Lombard (13)
Birkenhead High School

The Pit Pony

It's cold down here and dark
My body is racked with pain
I don't know how long I've been down here
But I do know I hate being down here.

There are noises; sinister noises
Noises I've never heard before
There are smells: awful smells
Smells I never have smelt and never want to smell again.

There is impenetrable darkness all around me
Swallowing me, enveloping me
It's coming closer, closer even closer
I can't see, it's terrifying.

There's a light coming, a bobbing faint light
There's a man, he's black with dust and smells of sweat
He's taking me somewhere
Somewhere I don't want to go.

He's talking to me, it's soothing, it's familiar
He's leading me
I can just see by the light in his hand
There's black rock everywhere, black walls, black floor. Black.

I've been brought to a mine!
I rear up, I do not like it
My hooves clatter against the floor and walls
I hit my head, I go down, it goes dark.

Every day my life is the same.
I'm tied to heavy loads of black rock
My coat's black, my mane is black
I don't even remember where I was before
Before I came here.
A mine, my home and my murderer.

Golfo Migos (13)
Birkenhead High School

A Precious Memory

A precious memory
Around five years ago
A magical wedding
I will never forget.

The last curl,
Twirled out of my hair.
I looked around
To see last minute preparations everywhere.

I stood up
And walked to the long mirror.
I felt like a princess,
Wearing a beautiful cream flower dress.

We stepped out of the bedroom,
One by one.
We all glided down the stairs,
To see in front of us a gathering of people.

I sat in my place
And watched with amazement.
The bride and groom,
Each placed rings on the other person's finger.

I smiled for the camera,
In the glorious gardens outside.
I jumped, leapt,
And danced all night long.

As the clock struck midnight,
I thought back,
This special day will stay with me,
Forever and ever.

Alice Somauroo (13)
Birkenhead High School

A Path Of Destruction

What a beautiful and serene sight,
The glistening sun quivering on the calm sea,
The locals enjoying a barbecue on the white sand,
On a winter's day that will never be forgotten.

The hustle and bustle of the city,
Was suddenly turned into a deathly silence,
When a colossal rumble echoed through,
The jewel that is Sri Lanka.

Screams and cries then followed,
A caterwaul of chaos,
As water came cascading through the streets,
Destroying everything in its path.

People drowned and buildings lost,
A sight for sore eyes,
And the horror of a little girl's face,
To see her mother being swallowed by the water.

A tidal wave of nightmares,
A land engulfed and gone,
All in one horrific day,
Such an inconsolable city.

No longer a beautiful and serene sight,
No sun shining in the sky,
No barbecues underway on the beach,
Just a grief-stricken land of sorrow.

Laura Savvas (13)
Birkenhead High School

Before It Began

As I walk through the ghost town,
Rubble, covering those who are lost forever
Gunshots and screams of pain
Echoing through the red, dusty street
I can still hear my mother's cries
As a bomb whistles through the grey skies.
Never to look or speak to me again.
Buried in the ruins of a house
I think to myself,
Why wasn't it me?
Silent
Dead.

I remember happy times
Before the war began,
Before men trudged into our towns,
Before many of us ran.
I remember my family,
Laughing and playing in our happy home.
The terrified, blank faces, when war was declared,
Not knowing they would never smile again.

Tears trickle down my face,
Making an insignificant stream,
Forever flowing through the human race.

Imogen Wilson (12)
Birkenhead High School

The Evening Sky

Shall I compare thee to an evening sky?
A line of delicate cloud streams across
The sun dips low after being so high
As the cloud floats off like a line of candyfloss
A warm glowing sun settles in for the night
Fluffy cloud drifts away into the black
Then disappears the last of the light
The clouds vanish over the railway track
Icy winds blow hard
The night turns cold
Day is shattered into shards
Night regains its gripping hold
The very next day this will happen again
The day undergoes this terrible pain.

Jake Roberts-Kendall (13)
Calday Grange Grammar School

Brutal War

I walk slowly down the dark trench,
Looking into his eyes, I see the pain he suffers,
My eyes fall to the floor, his eyes just shed pain,
I see the wounded, and the unmistakable dead.

I hear a merciless gunshot, I duck,
All I'm doing is delivering a poky little letter,
I hear a scream, then an uncanny silence,
We're one down for precious numbers.

I feel the pain in the air,
My face burning with anger, mistrust and starvation,
Feeling the pain in my heart I trudge on, weary and tired
The pain people suffer is unbearable.

I smell the blood, rotten and decaying,
There is the lingering smell of fired ammunition,
The stale smell of soldiers' sweat wandering round the trench,
War is a brutal place.

David Jones (12)
Calday Grange Grammar School

Grand National

I'm standing in the starting gate
I want to run, I really can't wait
Ding! There goes the starting bell
I'm off like a bullet, fast as hell
I'm leaving the rest of the group in my wake
The crowd need me to win, there's so much at stake
I may be old but I'm still the best
Hah! I'm miles ahead of the rest
Then all of a sudden I trip and I fall
And down comes horsey, rider and all
I look to my owner as he gives a scream
As I crash to the ground, so too does his dream.

Alex Clements (13)
Calday Grange Grammar School

A Prelude To Revelation

Mr Material chides the ethereal,
When his silver surrounded soul
Smiles at the coins in his eyes
Rather than the stars in the sky,
If fails to achieve the untold:
Truth is not gained for a measure of gold.
The gold: his real, his lust, his gist is
As tangible as the vapour rising
Above his reign of contentment.
Yet sometimes,
In the blue light of the moon
The silver melts away, his soul does swoon.
He chokes on his fate:
He is consumed by the desire to consume.

Aaron Bartels (17)
Calday Grange Grammar School

War

Warriors pacing,
To their enemy racing,
Clad in green
And holding me.

Justice stands
To all that demands
A peaceful life,
Clear of strife.

A grenade explodes,
The cliff face erodes,
Chunks of rock tumble
Crushing an enemy plane.

The cannons boom,
Making the tanks fall to doom.
The rifles crack,
Mighty bullets diving into warriors.

Blades clash,
Maces bash,
The world suffers,
As the warriors die.

A time of joy,
Destroyed by a simple decoy,
A wooden horse,
Full of these so-called enemies.

So what is this piece about?
War.

Danny Chu (11)
Calday Grange Grammar School

Season's End

Winter days are cold but comfortable
When wrapped up warm with my own inner bubble
These cold nights and short days
All year I wish that you could stay.

Spring is always next to come
Flowers blooming in the sun
End of hibernation for some creatures
The world now has more interesting features.

Summer is just around the bend
When spring is almost at an end
Summer's when the birds will sing
And to the sound you will want to cling.

Autumn is the time when leaves will fall
Lots of bare trees will stand so tall
A time of cold brown leaves or Hallowe'en
These four seasons are like a dream.

Scott Conway (12)
Calday Grange Grammar School

A Winter Morning

The sun struggles to warm the grey, bleak scene,
While the shivering shadows are statues in the dawn of day
Underneath the walls carrying mighty domes above
Their heads.

Cold cobbles drown under pearlescent pools,
Reflecting the beauty of the town,
And the lacklustre lamps light little lanes.
Down which mongrels scrape for scraps.

Small creatures of the night scurry back to their dens
And anxious dawn birds start to sing.
The clouds turn a rosy pink
As night turns to day.

Well-rested rich wake up to their butlers bringing tea,
The servants have been up for hours now.
Tired men go off to work,
Quiet monks chant in the church.
This happens on one winter morning.

Charlie Beech (12)
Calday Grange Grammar School

This Is The Day

This is the day you can't get in trouble
Without miserable people bursting your bubble
This is the day the world begins to see
And everyone knows you're not a baby
This is the day when everything changes
No one to protect you from all of life's dangers
This is the day you're made to grow up
You just wanna tell everyone else to shut up
This is the day no one can be mean
This is the day you turn thirteen.

Jack Starkey (13)
Calday Grange Grammar School

The Old Woman

Her eyes were as red as blood
The skin was battered and wrinkly
The dry crispy lips spoke few words
And her long pointy fingernails were like claws of a lion

Her long straggly hair was like a bramble bush planted on her head,
Spot-infested, her nose smelt very little,
People said her stench was like an old rotting dump.

Her small little mind was filled with terrible ideas
Old and dirty, her clothes hung off her like rags
You would have thought she was homeless
But this was the way she liked to live
She lived in an old, wind-battered shack
Swarming with creatures of all sorts.

Oh she loved her life,
One of the many people that did.

Jack Reed (13)
Calday Grange Grammar School

The Day

My dad went to work early one morning,
I was still in bed, I never saw him,
I got up, got washed and dressed,
I never thought I would feel so depressed.
It was a lovely sunny day,
I went to the playground and had a play.
The afternoon came with RE and maths,
Then I walked home at half-past,
I sat on the step waiting for Dad to come home,
By this time my mum had known,
Mum sat on the step next to me,
Then she made a happy plea.
I thought she was being silly,
But then Mum put on a serious face,
My nervous system shook all over the place,
She said Dad had left me and her,
For a second my life was a blur.
They were tears of sadness, not tears of joy,
What would happen to the poor young boy?

Matthew Ingram (11)
Calday Grange Grammar School

Nobody Comes Above

I wish that I could turn back time
I wish that I could do things right
Losing you would be committing a crime
Because, in my life you are the light.

Without you my life would be wrong
I'd miss you so much
Because, for you, I long
I'd feel like I'd lost a leg, and I was permanently on a crutch.

Everything about you
The best thing ever
All the things you do
I will love you forever.

I need to change the way I treat you
Otherwise I will lose my love
From this day I want to make you happy, not blue
In my heart, mind and soul,
Nobody
Comes
Above.

Jack Mooney (13)
Calday Grange Grammar School

My Brother's Room

His curtains are as yellow as the golden sun,
His mattress is as comfy as a dove's wing,
The wardrobes tower over you like prison walls,
The TV is as black as the night sky,
The carpet is like the desert sand,
His lamp is as bright as the thermite reaction,
You sink into the air cushion like a giant marshmallow,
His stereo is as loud as a giant's booming voice.

Alex Dodd (12)
Calday Grange Grammar School

Ambitions

To swim across the river Nile
To end up in a money pile
To be a Man United player
To be the country's highest mayor
Or simply be an outstanding chef
Be the greatest Premiership ref
To be the author of a great book
Win the lottery and have some luck
Or just be a teacher at a school
Be the owner of a swimming pool
I could travel all around the globe
Go to the highest star in a probe
Go out sailing in a grey sea mist
Or be at the top of the rich list.

Chris Hatton (13)
Calday Grange Grammar School

Revenge!

Over the shimmering valley,
The creature looks to the moon,
Strangely sweeping steadily,
Howling to a tune.

Across the groaning valley,
The blacksmith seeks revenge,
For there would be a battle,
In a place named Stonehenge.

The beast was like a werewolf,
But went on all fours,
It was an intelligent creature,
With extremely deadly claws.

The beast arrived to see,
The blacksmith had a crew,
With helmets, shields and bow and arrows,
And swords which they all drew.

In a desperate effort,
It tried to run away,
But the blacksmith's band,
Knew this was their day.

The blacksmith drew his wondrous sword,
To take the final blow,
The men gazed around the old dead corpse,
And watched his cold blood flow!

Callum Williamson (12)
Calday Grange Grammar School

Through The Eyes Of A Baby

A world full of colour, of smell, noise and taste
Learning all the things needed for life
Learning how to crawl, walk and run
Showing my family a whole lot of fun.

Cheeky grins to score brownie points
Pulling tongues to make them laugh
Standing up and grabbing keys
Cruising round and pinching knees.

I eat my food and drink my juice
I blow balloons that were for my birthday
I call for my dummy and call for my toys
Then I go to nursery to see the girls and boys.

Luke Marshall (12)
Calday Grange Grammar School

In The Dark

In the dark,
May be a bird,
It could be a shark,
It could be a word.

In the dark, no one knows,
Nothing goes in and no one shows.
No animals go in, no animals come out,
Once they go in, all you hear is a shout.

In the dark lies a horrible beast,
It comes from the west but comes from the east.
Its mighty roar can be heard from a mile,
If you shout back, it might take a while.

In the dark, nothing can be seen,
You can't see where you are going, or where you have been.
Wherever you go, you feel a dead end,
There is no fire to build, nor a letter to send.

Gregory Shone (13)
Calday Grange Grammar School

I Am A . . .

I am a table,
People sit on me,
I am not soft or cuddly
But I am as comfortable as can be.

I am a chair,
People draw on me,
They lean and swing,
And they don't learn a thing.

I am a bench,
People put gum on me,
They also read and eat their tea,
And this attracts lots of bees.

I am a train chair,
People do all sorts on me,
They can travel all around the world,
And they don't even think about me.

I am a car seat,
People sit on me,
I take them to and from everywhere,
While they go and do their thing.

Alex Rabot (12)
Calday Grange Grammar School

The Last Man

I'm the last man in
With fifteen to win
Eight balls left
Last man was out to a lofted heft

Their fastest bowler is steaming in
The fielders in the outfield are making such a din
The ball drops short, bouncing high
I hook it for six and watch it fly

The next one I leave and watch it pass by
The wicket keeper dives but watches it go for byes
Their leg spinner is slowly jogging in
Ripping it with some great spin.

Cooly stepping down the wicket I flick him away for four
One run more
Five balls left
Caught out to a lofted heft

A bowl out is an art for a craftsman
Stepping up there is their best batsman
He misses by a country mile
For this challenge I'll need all my cunning guile

I take middle out of the ground
It looks like we're trophy bound
Lifting the trophy high in the air
Now we have a pair.

Russell Smith (13)
Calday Grange Grammar School

God Versus Gravity

The argument of life's beginning
Between science and religion
Many lives have been lost over this lengthy debate
Between God, the big bang or maybe they relate.

Some say that one big rock came near
From that gravity upped a gear
And all the rocks pulled together
Held in place but not forever.

Others say that over seven days
God had some fun and started a craze
Religion landed on its head
They said it was the best thing since sliced bread.

I don't mind, whatever suits me
All the lies told and the hypocrisy
It makes me feel it could be either
But then again it could be neither.

Asher Winterson (13)
Calday Grange Grammar School

Starry Night

Shall I compare you to a starry night,
You make the lilac moon look like a lamp.
When I think of you, I fly through the wind like a winged kite,
Your voice echoes throughout like a very large amp.

You remind me of a rose with its petals falling to the floor,
One single red rose could fill my heart,
Could I have the key to the lock on your door?
Where I would find you there, as fresh as a fruit tart.

Is it that you have the brain of a computer
And the looks of a beautiful mermaid, swimming through the sea?
If only I could give you the gifts of gold, frankincense and myrrh
And then only you and me could be.

The rope between us is oh so tight,
Shall I compare you to a starry night.

Gabriel Alder (12)
Calday Grange Grammar School

The Sun

Upon the hill's edge it rests,
The golden orb lies in the sky,
As it looks down upon this Earth; the creatures,
The people, the land, the features.

When the morning comes,
The stars they dim,
And it shines with its golden rays,
For it we owe all beautiful days,

All of Earth talks,
While it remains mute,
Not a word it mutters in the azure skies,
As it watches over all of Earth's lies,

For it we have many names,
Sol, helios, the sun,
Yet we all know that it is there,
When we look upwards and glare,

The fountain of light flows,
Only disturbed by the clouds,
And for when it is grey,
It is harder to be content with that day,

But yet it vanishes every night,
To be replaced by the shadow of itself,
Now you see the reflections in the moon,
But you are safe in the knowledge that it will rise again soon.

Thomas Pickford (15)
Calday Grange Grammar School

Iraq

You see these men who go to war,
They all know what they're fighting for.
Yet little know they of impending doom,
While you sit in your living room.

These soldiers who journey to enlist,
To fight the fundamentalists.
But they don't battle mortal man
They battle religion with gun in hand.

Our boys, they fight for the United Kingdom,
The enemy fights for martyrdom.
Religion is stronger than the might of Man,
But we will fight it if we can.

They went too far, that fateful day,
When the WTC was blown away.
Religion is stronger than mortal Man
But we will fight it if we can.

Alex Harwood (12)
Calday Grange Grammar School

Imagination

Other people see a car
I see a rocket ship
And I travel to the moon and back.
Other people see the sun
I see an almighty light bulb
And every night I turn it off.
Other people see a tree
I see a huge man
And we talk.
Other people see a building
I see a giant slug
And it eats me.
Other people see a beach
I see a vast desert
And I ride on my camel.
Other people see sand
I see quicksand
And I sink.
Other people see nothing
I see everything.
Other people are boring.

Patrick Downie (11)
Calday Grange Grammar School

If Only

(When the aims of Rudyard Kipling's 'if' fail)

Boy, shadow of a man,
Your head missing, presumed dead, in the panic of those about you,
Your trust in them returned only by doubt and blame;
More than you would allow,
Your patience severely tested.

The risk never paid off,
They stole your winnings,
Threw lots and divided it between them,
It seems an age since you shook hands with triumph,
Disaster disguised itself and dominated your existence.

Ruled by dreams,
The contemplations in the cross-hair constantly preying on your mind,
The lies and hatred have poisoned you,
Contagious, a plague of despise,
Coating your subtle wisdom in blatant arrogance,

The truth you once spoke has become twisted into a deluded obsession,
One that you blindly follow day after day,
Minute after unforgiving minute,
A manic, relentless chant that you recite endlessly,

It could have been yours, a commoner among kings,
But you lost the race,
And looked on as the things you gave your life to,
Were brutally snapped in two and thrown to the ground,

'Build them up again,' says the voice, 'hold on.'
But what for?

Richard Powell (16)
Calday Grange Grammar School

The World Is Dead

What is wrong with us today? Places are burning, people are dying,
No peace on the streets and poor mothers are crying.
People are evil like monsters, there is no one to trust,
When will humanity find peace at last?
Why are we fighting to live, if we are just living to fight?
What are we trying to see when there is nothing in sight?
Why are we trying to give when no one gives us it back?
Why are we dying to live if we are just living to die?
The war of the worlds has not yet begun,
But we are fighting amongst each other like we are not one.

What happened to the world that we are meant to be in,
Rest and care as Heaven, which is what we are meant to have seen
But instead there are hostility and wars,
And people are scared behind their shut doors.
The world has truly changed,
Everyone is ashamed of the youth, because the truth seems strange,
But for us it's the worst,
We are left in the world which is cursed, and it hurts.
If only a saviour could come and help us clean up the mess,
Then people would look at the sky and shout, 'God bless!'

But we need to start acting right here, right now,
Nothing is impossible, so never bow down.
And if we start living the peaceful way,
We might just wake up one morning and say, 'What a beautiful day!'
I wish we could find a place free from sin,
So people can stop being horrible, hideous and mean.
The starving children might be able to get fed,
But until then, this world is regrettably dead.

Alex Clackson (16)
Calday Grange Grammar School

How Many More . . .?

One day I hope there will be peace,
Maybe all of the wars will cease.
How many more will die for their cause?
All we need to do is pause.

They promised to win our heart and mind,
But all they did was deceive mankind,
How many more generations will live by the knife?
Until conflict stops being a way of life.

Stop all the guns and stop the fights,
Then there will be no more sleepless nights.
How many more deaths will it take,
For us to realise the hate we make?

Will any road map, sanction or summit,
Cause the loss of life to plummet?
How many more bullets will be fired,
Until there are no more bodies in flags attired?

One day I hope we will live as one,
No more shall we hear the sound of the gun.
How many more broken hearts will it take?
We must stop for humanity's sake.

From this seed peace will grow,
But more seeds, we need to sow.
How many more words need to be said,
Until we realise how many are dead?

Raunak Poonawala (12)
Calday Grange Grammar School

My Cat, Natalie

My cat, Natalie, limps like she has one leg,
If she wants food, she sits to beg.
She is as deaf as a factory worker,
With earmuffs on all day.

She eats like a monster,
She snores like one too,
She sleeps like a sloth,
And she's hardly brand new.

Her face is like a lion's,
Her fur is like a rat's,
Her claws are like a bear's,
And she looks like a skeleton dipped in fur.

Her age is like a dinosaur,
Her smell is like a skunk,
Her eyes are wild like fire,
And she has ears like bats.

She circles round like she's on fire,
Finally the tornado has ceased,
She finally sits down,
And sleeps like a beast.

Seb Jones (13)
Calday Grange Grammar School

Hunter

I was padding along very happy after my kill
Then suddenly *bang* hundreds of bird flew out of the trees
I heard the cry of an elephant and the scream of buffalo
The vicious shot of a gun, had lives of many animals
I could hear the men roaring with laughter after taking
Innocent souls
My pack was discarded like rubbish
I didn't know what to do, I just froze
I had never experienced anything like this
Now the hunter is the hunted.

Iwan Bricker (12)
Calday Grange Grammar School

Poverty

Pain for the poor
No chances for the suffering
The world is against you
Just get nothing

A grain a day
The doctor's at bay
The problem is
No one can pay

School every month
If that at all
Teachers are limited
Waiting for the call

Jobs for the young
From ages of three
Work all day
And earn 2p

Clothes are scarce
There's nowhere to find them
There are dead bodies
What a horrible assignment

Scars all over them
On their hearts as well
Some struggle to walk
Life is hell

Those third world countries
What can they do
It's hard to understand
What these people go through.

Cameron Lea-Swain (12)
Calday Grange Grammar School

My Life

I used to have a good life,
Lots of food like fish,
That was served on my favourite dish,
My old life was no strife,

But now I'm alone,
Abandoned and in pain,
I don't know why they left me,
I feel as small as a bee,
But all I want is to be free,

So now you know,
What humans are like,
But I believe
That one day I will be found.

Jonathan Brown (12)
Calday Grange Grammar School

What It's Like To Be A Baby

Here I am, sitting in my pram
Mum's pushing me through the park
I'm feeling a bit thirsty, so I tell Mum that I'm thirsty
But it won't come out properly
I'm thinking, *I'm thirsty! I'm thirsty!*
But it just comes out as garbled rubbish
I wish I could speak properly
Mum never understands
I try to say things, but they never come out right
So I just cry and cry, and cry some more
Until Mum guesses what I want
We go home and Mum sits me on the couch and we watch Teletubbies
After a while she takes me up to my cot, but I'm wondering why
I'm not tired, I didn't even try to say that I'm tired,
So I cry again
Mum's getting irritated by me, but still I don't stop crying
Sleep's boring unless you get to sleep quickly
It's a waste of time
Mum doesn't give up and puts me in my cot
I cry but I can't get out, so I give up and go to sleep
I wake up later and Mum takes me downstairs to have dinner
Great! More baby food. It tastes disgusting
Like I've been sick and I have to eat it
So I spit it out, but Mum forces me to eat it or no Teletubbies
So I eat it
Then Dad comes home and he and Mum have dinner
After that they take me to bed
Dad reads me a story and I fall asleep
Ready to watch more Teletubbies and eat more horrid baby food
And another trip to the park in my pram.

Richard Lundy (12)
Calday Grange Grammar School

Poverty!

Poverty, poverty, poverty . . .
When will it ever end,
Taking things for granted,
Food, water and our friends.

Away in other countries,
Everyone sick and ill,
Nothing in this world can help them,
Not even the strongest pill.

No clothes, no clean water,
No food to eat,
Starving and thirsty,
And nothing on their feet.

Catching diseases day by day,
Illnesses getting worse,
They have nowhere to turn to,
It's as if they're under a curse.

As we leave food from our dinners,
Others will soon not exist,
We get so much in our lives,
It is like the poor have disappeared into the mist.

Living a bad life, we don't know what it's like,
How can people get so poor?
They all deserve so much more,
Poverty, poverty, poverty . . .

Stephen Jones (12)
Calday Grange Grammar School

The Manta Ray

The tropical sun lit sea,
A stunning glittered sight.
What a marvellous relaxing beauty
Shimmering with scattered light.

In the deep vivid blue,
Lie many marvellous features,
With decorative coral reefs,
And spectacular abnormal creatures.

From the fluorescent Regal Tang,
To should I dare say,
What could be an oblivious shark,
But really the manta ray.

Swimming is graceful fluidity,
A gigantic yet amazing being,
The manta flies magically,
Through sensing rather than seeing.

It journeys through vicious weather,
Unhindered by this tyrant roar,
In this rough external mayhem,
It glides across the sea floor.

But as the storm subsides,
And the sea is no longer obscure,
The full litheness of the manta ray,
Truly dazzles with awe.

Jacob Gourley (12)
Calday Grange Grammar School

Waking Up

The sun's warming hands stretch out to greet me,
The alluring flowers' scents billow towards me,
Appetising smells of breakfast seeping through the door.
My eyes open to see a felicitous figure with a beaming smile,
Urging me to eat such palatable foods that lay before me . . .

The wind's cold hands strike my icy cheeks
The pillow cover, exuding the bristling odours of alcohol,
The deafening silence surrounding me,
My eyes open to see a tyrannous Machiavellian man before me,
Ferociously beating me,
Screams of pain and melancholy . . .

Matthew O'Malley-Clark (12)
Calday Grange Grammar School

The Radioactive Pig

The radioactive pig wears a trendy wig
And trots along the street to a funky beat,
But his skin glows green instead of pink
So he makes up for it with a wink.
We ask him why oh why oh why
He doesn't roll in mud or eat so much pie.
So he says, 'I'm no ordinary pig, I'm a wicked, ravin'
Party pig and some say I drive like the stig.'

The radioactive pig lives on my street
And every day he eats shredded wheat.
Then he goes to work in his flashy car
As the one and only pig superstar.

Greg Cawthorne (11)
Calday Grange Grammar School

Homeless Insanity

The pointless chatter of happy families drifting over my head.
A dirty look every few minutes,
I am less than a person, deserving to die.
I am used to the cold, although I don't know it,
Not just on the outside but the inside as well.
Love I have lost, opportunities wasted, thrown away my education,
But now I understand everything.
Wanted by nobody, reduced to eating out of bins,
If I could only start again.
I have no friends to sustain me,
Just myself and insanity to contend with.
If only the children who pass me, knew how lucky they are.
What I would give for a hot meal, a warm bed and new clothes on my back.

In my heart I know that I'm dreaming,
But without dreams I'd struggle to survive.
Through the cold, harsh nights I huddle in fear,
For I'm just a child inside, fragile and scared.
How long will I live? that scared voice asks,
I find I don't care, nothing matters anymore.
Forced to live out my days, crouched in this dark corner,
They say life is short but for me nothing's longer.
I'm dirty, disgusting, lying in filth,
My bleak dream world overpowering.
Outcast of society, failure in all fields,
Living off false ideas, a parasite,
A rodent deserving to die.

Alexander Quirk (12)
Calday Grange Grammar School

Through The Eyes Of A Soldier

I dropped to my hands and knees,
As I slowly crawled across the sandy, pebbly turf,
Dragging my gun through the gusty winds,
I heard a gunshot echoing.
I scrambled to my feet as I moved into the dark forest.
My pacing steps slowed as I advanced further and further
Into the forest,
A chill shivered down my spine.
As the darkness grew thicker and thicker,
It was as if a blanket of the midnight sky descended
down onto Earth.
It was as frightening as the Devil approaching you,
And dark beyond expectations.
I made it to where I heard the gunshot,
As I overlooked a man on the ground.
He was just lying there, choking on his own saliva.
As a tear shed from his bloodshot eyes,
It trickled down his almost lifeless face, dropping onto
the cold ground.
How horrible, to watch a man crying over his own tortured death.
He drew me near . . . wiping the saliva from his mouth,
With his breath he uttered, 'Dulce et decorum est . . .'
As I finished,' . . . pro patria mori.'
As he lay there, so peacefully, I walked away, awaiting my fate . . .

Joshua Colton (13)
Calday Grange Grammar School

I Love Football

I love football, cheering on my team,
It's just like being in an action-packed dream.

I love football, shooting at goal,
Or taking a corner, standing next to the pole.

I love football, singing the anthem,
A thrilling feeling in my tum.

I love football, watching them score,
Joining in with the crowd's loud roar!

I love football, running around,
The ball at my feet, on top of the ground.

I love football, getting mad at the referee,
It was definitely a foul, he obviously can't see!

I love football, even if I lose,
I'll just ignore the sideline boos.

I love football, when I beat the opposition,
Scoring lots of goals in my up-front position.

I love football, watching 'Match of the Day'
Having at look at what Lineker has to say.

I love football, putting my skills to the test,
Win or lose, I tried my best!

Calum Edward (12)
Calday Grange Grammar School

Wednesday

I am awakened, cold and shaken,
My witching eyes find smoky bacon,
Feral screams rip open the silence,
I cower from the impending violence,
The doors fling open and I am free,
I look back at the box and skip joyfully,
This new box is tall and towering,
I find myself searching and scouring,
The only way to escape this scene,
Is to run and jump from the trampoline.

I land in a lake; it's murky and brown,
I can't swim and start to frown,
Crocodiles lie in wait,
I could distract them with some bait,
I look around the box I'm in,
And I spot a small chicken,
I grab the bird and slice its throat,
I hear the sound of a mountain goat,
Running to the sheep-like sound,
I begin to hurtle to the ground,
This innocent goat is but a trap,
It's really a lion and a big one at that,
It's growling, slobbering, carnivorous jaws,
Grip my face and more blood pours,
In this box I will surely die,
I let out a sorry sigh.

Oliver Spinney (12)
Calday Grange Grammar School

History

The ancient, old grey steps beckon me
Age-old entrance calls me with a spell
The rotting, rampaging row of wall I see
A great battle happened here where I sleep.

Stone-cold walls are cackling madly
There are monsters lurking behind the black curtain
Shiny magic flows from a staff, but sadly
The great magician is lost.

Broken swords, shattered limbs of once-great nations
Evil here has conquered hearts of good men
Bollards I see again, back is the station
Endless times I had been here
But this time I had been into *history.*

Gokhul Raj Ramakrishnan (12)
Calday Grange Grammar School

In The Box

(Based on 'Magic Box' by Kit Wright)

In the box, contrasting colours blind the barmy parrot.
A jungle of colours and multicoloured cows and a sea
Of strawberry smoothie.
Flying in the curly and colourful sky are penguins
In formation, drinking milkshake.
Cars racing along at speed with jimbobbalooey
Winning.

In the box, a poster of Elvis Presley is dancing to
James Brown.
Outside I see a multicoloured missile with a white mouse
On the end.
Inside, Barney the Dinosaur is sunbathing as if he is outside.
A pink elephant is on my roof doing an Irish jig.

In the box is the Empire State building with a platypus on top.
There is a giant iPod at the bottom with lots of polka dots on it.
Flying pigs break the airspeed record. Who said pigs can't fly?
Blind parrots smoke pieces of paper.

In the box, burning, hot, blind baboons bounce boingly.
'Peace,' say the hippies with their multicoloured robes.
A ruler is doing its balancing act on top of a rugby ball.
Little see-through mice scramble squeakily.

Sam Bangura (13)
Calday Grange Grammar School

Boxing

I'm in the ring throwing punches
My opponent's teeth shatter and his jaw crunches,
I drop my guard, what a mistake
As he performs the double take,
Blood splatters from my face
My nose is on my forehead and my teeth are all over the place,
I suddenly hit the deck,
Oh! how I look an awful wreck,
Why, oh why did I get out of bed?
I could've been snuggled up with my bear called Ted.

Thomas Sanders (13)
Calday Grange Grammar School

Politics

George Bush is such a bore
All he thinks of is war, war, war!

Tony Blair is Bush's singer
As he's wrapped around his warmongering finger

Jacques Chirac never put men in the trenches
Instead he has them on Paris benches

In Baghdad there are scenes of slaughter
Father killing brother's daughter

If this onslaught carries on
The very last traces of hope will be gone

Our precious world is going into disrepute
This will not be swift and cute

All this disruption's gone off like a gun
Politics, shmolotics, look what it's done.

Roy Asterley (12)
Calday Grange Grammar School

Should I Compare You To A Red Sunset?

Should I compare you to a warm red sunset?
Your voice is as extraordinary as the sweet bird's song,
I'm like a fish, can't let you go, I'm stuck in a net,
I've been waiting for you for so, so long.

When I'm with you time goes so quick,
Your face is as warm as the heavens above,
Our friendship and love are as strong as a diamond brick,
You're as swift and as elegant as a flying white dove.

You're as cuddly as a furry brown bear,
When we first kissed I went into a dream,
Whenever I see you, I always stare,
You're as hot as a sun's beam.

I want to be with you forever and ever
Me and you match together!

Daniel Lees (13)
Calday Grange Grammar School

Everything Is Wrong With The World

Everything that is wrong with the world,
Nuclear bombs being made in Iran,
Iraq the gravestone for British pride,
Britain a once prosperous nation,
Now with a generation they'd rather forget,

People working till their seventies,
Parents getting younger and younger,
Children getting 'stupider',
Authority finding prisons for first offenders,
But letting serial paedophiles run loose,

Everything that is wrong in the commons,
Labour getting paid for peerages,
Lib Dems leading with a pensioner,
The Conservatives, aka the posh party,
So who to choose at election time, will we ever know?

Robert Mallon (13)
Calday Grange Grammar School

Champions League Final

We go out for the kick off
The atmosphere is great
The ref blows his whistle
And off goes the match.

Straight away they score
And we are all in shame
It is now the thirty-ninth minute
And they have scored again.

We use up all our energy
And go up to attack
Now they are on the run
And Crespo lobs the keeper.

We go in for half-time
And have a huge team talk
AC Milan kick off
But Gerrard gets the ball.

Garcia crosses it in
And Gerrard gets the goal
But shortly after that
Smicer has a shot.

And the next minute you know
It's in the back of the net
They kick off once again
Suddenly goes down Gerrard.

'Penalty,' shouts the ref
Alonso steps up and
It gets rebounded
And Alonso scores to equalise.

Now it is penalties
And Liverpool have won.

Max Cooper (11)
Calday Grange Grammar School

My Mum's 40th

It was the 16th of March
My mum's big 40
She was really excited
For the day tomorrow.

My dad was broke
Spending money on my mum
While my mum was relaxing
Right by the sun.

The bus did arrive
Our friends were amazed
They were startled
And very dazed.

When we arrived
At Thornton Hough
The chauffeur came
And took our stuff.

'This party's amazing
It's really cool'
My mum said,
'Even a pool.'

After the party
We all fell asleep
Upstairs in our penthouse,
Not a peep.

Conor Flanagan (12)
Calday Grange Grammar School

Kids

Posh kids have extravagant suits
Poor kids have old rags
Chav kids have Burberry
With the faint smell of fags.

Posh kids have lots of money
Poor kids have to beg
Chav kids have to steal it
From their next-door neighbour Meg.

Posh kids have mansions
Poor kids are homeless
Chav kids live on estates
Which are in a gigantic mess.

Posh kids go to private schools
Poor kids try to learn at home
Chav kids are always bunking off
Because they prefer to be left alone.

Posh kids play golf
Poor kids are lucky to play anything at all
Chav kids don't play any sport
Because they're always fighting over football.

Posh kids have happy families
Poor kids can't even get a wife
Chav kids have kids at sixteen
But who has the best life?

Roger Smith (12)
Calday Grange Grammar School

What Will Happen?

Will today be good or bad?
Will people today be happy or sad?
Who will I meet today?
Will the clouds be white or grey?
I wonder what will happen.

Will the trees sway and swing?
I hope this bee won't give me a sting.
Will the sun start shining soon?
Or will we see the shining moon?
I wonder what will happen.

Douglas Franklin (11)
Calday Grange Grammar School

Pub Mockery

(Based on 'Jabberwocky' by Lewis Carroll)

'Twas Sunday and the drunken blokes,
Did swear and mumble in the pub,
All drinking were the tipsy folk,
And outdated was the grub.

'Beware the Flabbydrunk my son,
The mouth that drinks, the breath that stinks,
Beware the Lagerlad and shun
The Dipsomaniac.'

He took his trusty cider in hand,
Long time the obese foe he sought,
Then rested he by the lavatory,
And sat a while in thought.

And as in foolish thought he stood,
The Flabbydrunk with eyes for port,
Came wobbling through the flooded loo,
And gibbering as it came.

One two! One two! And whack and whack
The cider bottle went crack! Crack!
He left it dead and with its wallet,
He went a-skipping back.

'And have you slain the Flabbydrunk?
Come to my arms my boozed up boy.'
'O fabulous day, hurrah! Hurrah!'
He chortled in his joy.

'Twas Sunday and the drunken blokes
Did swear and mumble in the pub,
All drinking were the tipsy folk,
And outdated was the grub.

Solomon Wrathall (12)
Calday Grange Grammar School

Midnight

The harvest moon is bright white,
Shining down like a gleaming light.

The midnight shadow makes me shiver,
All I can hear is the sound of a river.

As I walk through the streets
I start to get the creeps.

The wind blows the trees
And is cold enough to make me freeze.

I can see my home,
Even so, I feel alone.

I came back too late,
I shouldn't have stayed out with my mate.

A car drove past,
Then I started to run fast.

I was struggling to see in the dark,
Then, suddenly I heard a dog bark.

I reached my house,
Making sure I was as quiet as a mouse.

I will never stay out until midnight,
The journey home was too much of a fright!

Alex Smith (12)
Calday Grange Grammar School

A Pencil Poem

I'm here sitting on a chair
Watching the pencil just lying there
It is round, yellow, as bright as the sun
With a rubber on the end for erasing what's been done
I shall send this round, yellow pencil with the rubber on the end
To my brother and sister and whole family tree
For this little pencil is very special to me.

Luke Challoner (12)
Calday Grange Grammar School

On RuneScape

RuneScape is an online game,
Lots of people think it's lame,
I for one play on it,
My guy has a cool shiny kit.

RuneScape is set in the past,
Full of spells which a player can cast,
Swords, shields and axes too,
Beasts roar and cows moo.

Make a living and get rich,
Become a hero or be a witch,
Watch out for scammers,
Who will take your stuff,
Or fight a friend who thinks they're tough!

Joash Knight (11)
Calday Grange Grammar School

The Monster . . .

This monster bathes in the deep,
All she likes to do is sleep,
This monster has eyes of flames,
She calls other people names,
This monster has a jagged tail,
It's half as long as a whale!
This monster has hair on her head,
I think it is a mop instead,
This monster's twice as strong as me,
I am a weakling you see,
This monster lives in my house,
She likes to wear a purple blouse,
This monster has scaly skin,
She has some food upon its chin,
This monster likes to lie in bed,
But sometimes what she does instead,
Is that she likes to eat things whole,
She can slip down a chocolate Swiss roll,
This monster has the name of Rosa,
She really is quite a poser,
This monster is my skin and blister,
This monster is my *little sister!*

Bramwell Jungnitz (12)
Calday Grange Grammar School

Performing

The joy of performing,
The angst if being boring,
Surely there is no better feeling?

Whether it's script reading,
Or maybe fake bleeding,
It's simply superbly amazing,
The flashy lights,
The theatre-filled nights,
The crowd.
The thundering applause,
The extremely good cause,
That is entertainment.

The nerves before,
The irresistible lure,
Of performing to me,
Like a sailor loves the sea.
Anyone can perform,
Whether in a theatre,
Or college dorm.

What's not to like?
Nothing is wrong,
But all is right.

Thomas Martin (12)
Calday Grange Grammar School

Is This The End Of My World?

I feel your touch of power
I see your face of beauty
I hear your voice of charm
Is this the end of my world?

I feel your hand of velvet
I see your legs of splendour
I smell your scent of happiness
Is this the end of my world?

I feel your breath of ice
I see your hands of sensitivity
I taste your lips of glory
Is this the end of my world?

I feel your hair of smoothness
I see your feet of radiance
I smell your hands of jasmine
Is this the end of our world?

Alex Greenhalf (13)
Calday Grange Grammar School

The Last Train Home

'Ladies and gentlemen, the train to Paddington Square will be leaving
shortly . . .'

I fidget nervously in the seat,
The people around me dwell in a blissful ignorance,
Oblivious of the coming storm.
Today our journey ends.

My bag feels heavier than usual,
A fire inside waiting to be unleashed on the world,
Sending the embers of justice far and wide,
Today I will show them our power.

For honour, for Allah,
I casually open my rucksack,
Fingers delicately stroke the weapon of God.
Today the infidels' fate is sealed.

An outcast to my own people,
I do not 'represent' them,
Only those that follow the true path deserve to be saved,
Today they will see what a fanatic can do.

Destroy the lies, the hate, the news,
Destroy the life I cannot choose.
Destroy the politicians who don't give a damn.
Destroy these people - it's part of His plan.

On the Day of Judgement only the righteous can be saved,
The 'innocents' have had their chance to repent,
I flick the switch, the beacon of hope has arrived,
My time has come . . .
And so has yours.

Tom Browning (15)
Calday Grange Grammar School

I Don't Like Politics!

I don't like politics, politics doesn't like me,
I don't like presidents or ministers of any sort you see,
They have too much power and don't use it well,
All their problems seem to end in a bombshell!

Wars, guns, bombs, slaves, soldiers ready to serve,
The big men feast, drink and banquet, while the poor starve.
The greedy have no thought for the hurt, ill or dead,
This world is a mess cos it's governed by stupid big heads!

The ozone layer is melting, species dying,
The rich laughing, the refugees crying,
Get rid of the presidents; that's the key
I don't like politics, politics doesn't like me.

Alex Thomas (12)
Calday Grange Grammar School

A Fading World

What is happening in the world today?
Violence, drugs and death,
Innocence slaughtered, hopes destroyed,
Only if we could reset the time.
I bet the world was a better place without electricity,
Industry and wealth,
There was no abuse, or crime, or war,
Toward Mother Nature's fading health.

Why is pollution taking over the once so peaceful Earth?
Chimneys, noise and smog,
Forests demolished, lives been lost,
Only if we could reset the time.
I bet the world was a better place without destruction,
Vehicles and tools,
There was no devastation, or din, or fumes,
Large machines use mankind as fools.

What is happening in the world today?
Death, destruction and loss.

Daniel Hay (12)
Calday Grange Grammar School

The Eagle

He flies majestically over the world,
Surveying its contents over his hooked beak,
Soaring through the endless blue sky effortlessly,
His wingtips touch the heavens.

He spies a movement in the grass miles below,
The king folds back his great wings and drops like a stone,
Through the clouds the magnificent bird hurtles,
Down to the earth below.

He shoots along like a stone from a sling,
Glistening talons seize the unsuspecting vole,
Beating his immense wings he rises once more,
Into the evening sun.

Tim Gordon (12)
Calday Grange Grammar School

Save It - The World

Wouldn't the world be a better place,
If Man stopped wiping each other off its face,
To unite and help each other when in need,
Not make them pay for every deed!

The needless wars; the loss of life,
But no, people are left in grief and strife.
So save the world - and each other;

Treat everyone like sister, like brother . . .

Avrah Abraham (11)
Calday Grange Grammar School

Life And Death

Life is life, but what is life?
Death is death but what is death?
This I don't know but I'll tell you what I think.

I believe life is for living it to the full,
It's also for fun, excitement, fantastic adventure.

Life can also be like a balloon full of sadness as well,
Life's to cry on shoulders then to carry on.

Life's for forgiveness and to forget like pencil and rubber,
But also to remember and relive good times as well.

Life is a fragile bubble
Which can easily be popped.

And then death is next,
Now this one I don't know a lot about, but I'll try my best.

I believe death is for resting in total peace,
Also with no wars or pain.

Death is like a snake weaving through thoughts
To enjoy perfect memories.

Death is for watching people enjoy life,
It's to remember how you enjoyed it as well.

James Cavanagh (13)
Calday Grange Grammar School

The Storm's Way

Through the eye of the storm,
Whirling, twirling,
Sucking everything into it,
Whirlwind howling like a young wolf cub,
Full of energy,
Fierce, not stopping for anyone or anything in its path,
Destruction as the target of life,
Sucking the life of landmarks,
A swirling, long, mad black hole,
Crazy, out of control,
Getting angry and mean,
The farmhouse is gone for its feasting,
Black holes snack,
Rapping and tapping,
Crunching up cars,
The sea is rough,
Coming over the wall,
Crashing against the rocks,
Ships in peril,
What can we do?
This storm has its unstoppable and curious way!

Ben Ward (12)
Calday Grange Grammar School

Teenage Years

Teenage romance,
So full of chance,
And fate,
And getting home late,
With your hair in a mess,
And the telltale creased dress,
Slamming doors and floods of tears,
Full of emotion,
Teenage years.

Fashion and make-up,
Argue then break up,
The world itself has come to an end,
But you're out the next night, again with your friends,
Whispers of cheating,
And secretly meeting,
Mini skirts and crop tops,
Kerrang and Top of the Pops,
Fun but fleeting,
These teenage years.

Facials and football,
Texting and phone calls,
Exams, stress and strife,
The trials and tribulations of teenage life,
Every new boyfriend is 'the one'
With every break up you can't go on,
That is why every adult you ask will reply,
Thinking of all the tears that they had to cry,
'I wouldn't be a teenager again,
But I'd do my early twenties.'

Katherine Wilkinson (16)
Calday Grange Grammar School

That Special Feeling

That feeling, that magical feeling,
It's the lottery that you've won,
You're left astounded and unbelieving,
You feel like number one,
Like an eagle in the sky,
You're almost touching the stars,
So ecstatic you can fly,
To an illustrious world afar,
Weird, wonderful and wicked ideas echo around your head,
You're soaring over the moon,
Heavier than a ton of lead,
Is your newly found fortune,
It means absolutely everything to you,
Now you can do what you've always wanted to.

Liam Hughes (12)
Calday Grange Grammar School

Steven Gerrard

My favourite footballer is Steve Gerrard,
He's much better than Frank Lampard!

He can score goals from anywhere,
He really has got lots of flair.

The marvellous Liverpool is his team,
To play for them was his dream.

He should be skipper of Eng-er-land,
Terry just beat him to the legendary band.

For Liverpool he wears number eight,
Every game he plays he's great.

He scores lots of goals from outside the box,
Steven Gerrard really rocks.

For England he's number four,
From him you could ask no more.

He's the greatest at passing on the Earth,
£40 million is his worth.

He can hammer the ball exceedingly hard,
He rarely gets a yellow card.

He covers every blade of grass,
He's definitely top of my class.

He's even got an MBE,
Given by her majesty.

We battered Chelsea by two goals to naught,
The blues' fans were utterly distraught.

When he plays Liverpool always win,
Then 'The Kop' make such a din!

Nick Jones (12)
Calday Grange Grammar School

A Puppy

The puppy is born,
As it first sees daylight,
The miracle of dawn,
As the puppy yawns.

As smooth as fur,
With its glistening shiny hair,
Someone take me home,
Where I can be loved.

Look at me,
And then you will see,
How cute I am,
And how soft I am.

As I first went out,
I felt so scared,
I can't believe how far I walked,
And had so much fun playing on,
The bright green grass.

I bounced and pounced
For over an hour,
I love the field,
I call it my playhouse.

I love all my friends and family
And my treats and toys,
I am only a puppy,
That's who I am.

Bethanie Garrity (11)
Cowley Language College

Dolphin

The dolphin glides
As if it owns the sea,
Like a king owning its castle
The huge dolphin
Swims as fast as a cheetah running across the grass.
The bottle-nosed dolphin swims elegantly,
Like a princess looking for her prince,
The dolphin is grey and dull,
Just like a huge rain cloud about to burst
Its raindrops on the Earth.
The blue dolphin is the same as the waves crashing at the walls.
The dangerous world where dolphins live,
Is a mess with empty bottles, like the tip.
The slimy dolphin,
Just like snail slime.

Rebecca Maddocks (11)
Cowley Language College

Dreamer

Come to me
In my dreams
Where we can be alone together
Hold me close, hold me tight
I'll see you clearly in the night.

Close your eyes, and think of me
I'll do the same
Halfway between is where we'll meet
You'll feel me breathe
And you will see
That I believe this is Heaven for me.

Lover can't you see
This is all so real for me
Feel my heartbeat
Hear my soul
And know that I
Will never
Let
Go.

Alex Taylor (15)
Cowley Language College

The Dungeon

Dark in the dungeon are things that creep
Dark in the dungeon are bones that sleep
Dark in the dungeon are swords and shields
Dark in the dungeon is flesh and blood
Dark in the dungeon it's haunted and wet
Dark in the dungeon are ghosts of soldiers on patrol
Dark in the dungeon are the heads of fallen knights
Dark in the dungeon are the messages in blood of defeated
prisoners.

Terry Price (11)
Cowley Language College

The Lonely Kitten

Terrified like a mouse
I used to live in a house
I am so skinny and so thin
I could even eat a biscuit tin.

You will find me in a park
It is like I have no heart
All I want is a home
Sometimes I feel so very alone.

Alice Donellan (12)
Cowley Language College

The Table

Please don't stick things on me
Don't pull my legs off, it will make me cry
Don't make fun of my short legs
I am a dog running through the field
Don't graffiti on me, it will hurt my eyes
Please repair me if you hurt me or snap me
People think I'm hard but I'm really soft
They don't understand I have feelings too
Don't put coffee or tea marks on me
Use a coaster or a tablecloth
Clean up your mess if you spill something on me
When you are working on me please don't press on me too hard
When you eat on me make sure you don't burn me
Don't put loads of things on me or I will collapse on the floor
If you don't clean me I will go rusty
I am as hard as nails
I am wooden as a wooden door
I shine like diamonds in the midnight sky.

Jade Malone (12)
Cowley Language College

A Lonely Dog

Lonely heart slowly sinking
Down, down, never-ending
Help me please, I need some TLC
And maybe a home
And people to love me
Do you know what I am . . .?

Cerys Edden (11)
Cowley Language College

The Dog

A smelly, small, short and shaggy dog
With water coming down his ears
Like a dripping drainpipe.

The dog is black
Like a vampire's cave
A vampire
Coming to eat me!

A dog in a dark park barking
Like a tiger coming
Towards me!

Sehriban Yurdakurban (11)
Cowley Language College

The Cat

Fluffy black like a dark rain cloud
A cat is like a ginger biscuit, you can eat it all up
A tiny cat climbs up the tree like a tiger in the jungle
A cat is the black night sky, looming over me cheekily.

Hannah Norton (11)
Cowley Language College

The Shark

A shark is a bright light of thunder
Whatever you say you are going under.

His eyes are like bullets in the night
It hunts its prey like a bear on ice.

A shark has got a sense of smell like humans.

Matthew Graham (11)
Cowley Language College

The Dolphin

Floating around under the sea
To wait for a play friend to play with me
Searching for food
I am just in a happy mood!
Moving my tail, going up and down
If anyone is coming then I will frown
Meeting up with family
Running around and chasing others
I'll search the ocean looking for my brothers
Chasing little fish left and right
Turning back out of sight
Somersaults, backwards and forwards
Watching English species
And if you tell me off then I will come to pieces
All these boats and ships on the sea
Seem so peculiar to me.

Laura Southward (11)
Cowley Language College

The Tiger

The tiger is a pouncing dude.
The tiger is bouncing with joy.
The tiger is a spear of light,
He will attack, like a maniac
He sneaks on its prey slowly as it's moving
His eyes are like the moon piercing through the trees,
He soars like an eagle across India in search of his kill
He snarls like a cat running through the night.

Chris Ellis (11)
Cowley Language College

The Penguin

I live in a very cold place
I have icicles hanging off my face
But if I get too hot I will shrivel up and die
And because I'm a penguin I can't fly
I wibble, wobble across the snow
Slipping and sliding as I go.

Daniel Conway (11)
Cowley Language College

Too Fast, Too Furious

Revving up the engine
Accelerating fast
I'm always changing gear because I don't want to be last
The wind blows on my forehead which is the windscreen
I've been battered by my owners because they are mean
I need petrol to go and money to pay
I'm going to scream whether or not all day
I'm precious, I've got jewels at the front of me and rubies at the back of me.
I can see all day just as long as you stay out of my way.

Ryan Thornley (11)
Cowley Language College

Aeroplane

He bunny-hops into the sky like a big fluffy bunny rabbit.
As he gets above the clouds he looks like he is on top of Mount Everest.
When he gets sky-high he looks at the view around him
He sees aeroplanes flying very quick like cars on the motorways.
He never runs out of fuel because he loves having drinks at airports.
He loves looking for aeroplanes, it reminds him he is not alone.
He likes passengers but sometimes he thinks there is about
Fifty kilograms on top of him.
When he lands he feels like he fell off a two-mile-high brick wall
Because the impact when he lands feels like he has broken his legs.

Daniel Bamber (11)
Cowley Language College

The Doctor

Doctors are like vicious monsters
They are vile, mean and cruel
Sometimes they come into your school
They are dangerous dragons with a fiery breath of death
Their breath is like an underground sewer.

They are never nice
And they speak like mice
They are like a destructive deadly bomb ready to explode
With a big, bad, bold red face
You'll be in the right place
If you are ill and it's really bad
Don't mess with the doctor or he'll get mad.

In the waiting room it is dark, gloomy and scary
The woman is a zombie waiting to call you
You can screw her eyeballs out
While you are hanging about
Her skin is a mummy's mouldy bandages.

Her breath is a mouldy cup of sour milk
That looks like white and green silk
Beware of the doctor, he is dangerous and mean
He has equipment that will make you squirm and scream.

James Bushell (11)
Cowley Language College

I Am A Book

I am a book, you turn my pages all the time
Like a door opening and shutting
You rip my pages and break my spine from head to toe
You squash me up on a bookshelf
You let me get all dusty
I hold a lot of information
That you do not want
You wedge bookmarks in-between me
Why do you treat me so badly?

Alison Lovell (11)
Cowley Language College

The Lonely Kitten

A lonely heart,
Sat in a cage,
With no one to adopt me.
I'll be in a park,
Against a tree,
But all I want is a home.

No one will take me
Because I'm too small.
I may be skinny
But I'll show them all.

People who hate me,
Will beat me up,
So I run away and stay
By a garbage can.

Jay Smith (11)
Cowley Language College

Through The Eyes Of A Child Going To An Exam

Today is the day and I don't want to go
I'm going to do really bad I just know
My mum said, 'You're going to do great
So hurry up and don't be late.'

I've got butterflies in my belly
I wish I could stay at home and watch the telly
I've got an exam
And I'm stuck in a traffic jam.

I hope, maybe, I can stay at home
Even though I will be alone
Oh no, I'm at school,
My mum is such a fool.

I'll have to do the test
Who knows, maybe I'll be better than all the rest.

Kerry Highcock (14)
Cowley Language College

My Dad

If I could just turn back time,
To that day,
The day my dad went away,
If I was just awake to say goodbye,
To my dad before he went to the sky.

Two days before he went away,
We went to Saints' big game,
We beat Wigan in the Challenge Cup,
Oh, if only I was up.

If I was just up to say goodbye,
It wouldn't be as hard to see him die,
We had the best ever weekend,
And my love for him will never end.

Marc Webster (13)
Cowley Language College

Do I Deserve This?

Do I deserve this?
I am just a girl
In this cruel, injust, bitter world
I have eyes; I have a nose, ten fingers and ten toes
Do I deserve this?
As I walk down the road
Dodging the daggers that my fan club throw
My cold hands trembling, anticipating, shaking
As with their stone hearts, they plot the next attack
And what will they do once I have gone?
Disappear, non-existent, extinct, like they want
Another victim, another crime
Another innocent life shattered by their prejudiced minds
Do I deserve this?
I am no different
Yet they scratch, they claw, they bite
An insult to animals to describe them as this
Like scavenging vultures throughout the night
Their hatred words batter my dirty black skin
Bruised, bleeding from deep within
As an impure tear dribbles from my bloodshot eyes
I scream in fear and the world begins to cry
Their entertainment is here
Their biased lives are bliss
I stumble alone into the darkness
I do not deserve this.

Jessica Graham (15)
Cowley Language College

Global Warming

I give you water so you can drink,
And land on which you live.
So take a minute and just think,
In return what do you give?

Light in the day,
Waves in the sea,
Who makes this possible?
Yes, it's me!

I give you warmth, love and care,
And snow that falls soft and white.
My body, I let everyone share,
So how come you don't treat me right?

Raindrops so fresh,
Green grass on the hill.
Because of these fumes
I feel ill!

I give you animals which run free,
And a calm, cooling breeze.
Look to the sky and you will see,
I provide heat so you don't freeze.

Mountains so wide,
Trees so high,
All will be gone,
Once I die!

I give you everything you could need
But you pollute me every day.
It runs through my heart as a poisonous weed.
Who are you to waste my life away?

Jake Hughes (16)
Cowley Language College

The Story Of Ariel

As I was trapped in a tree,
My new master set me free.
I love Prospero from my heart,
I have always loved him from the start.

As the tempest he did describe to me,
He then reminded me that he set me free.
So to that I did the tempest,
Which the lightning fried them like a
Chicken breast.

As my master sets his traps,
Will he set me free . . .? Perhaps
As he finishes and lets me go,
I was going to say no.
For I love my dear Prospero.

Gemma Adair (13)
Cowley Language College

At The Gates Of Heaven

My eyes are blinded by pure white light.
I feel soft silky material flowing in a breeze against my innocent skin.
I hear doves in the distance chirping and I hear water dripping,
I smell a forest somewhere, though I cannot see one.

My body is moving, however my muscles do not contract
or mechanise,
I turn my head around and see waxen wings attached to me!
Up ahead I see a figure all in white, so white it hurts my angelic eyes,
I notice that I am not on ground but between blackness and stars.

I become nervous and my heart pounds quicker and harder,
I hear a voice, 'Don't worry, you're safe here my friend.'
I try to move myself but I'm locked in my own body,
I look forward, and there are huge gates, golden and cleaned
to perfection.

The figure opens its hands and the gates open magically,
This figure is wearing pure white and has waxen wings,
The presence of this figure is queer and eerie
Once again my jaw moves my helpless body beyond the
mysterious gates.

I feel as if I have met this figure before it holds its hands out,
I put my hands onto its, and it says to me,
'Have thou yet discovered the meaning of life?'
In my head I wonder if this is God.
It replies automatically, 'It is God.'

I tell God that I think life is just a test, about each individual,
If you're good and have your sins pardoned, you go on to Heaven
Or if you're evil and sadist, you go down into Hell.
I believe.
Amazingly my skin cracks open and my spirit pours out.
God says to me, 'You are welcomed here my friend.'
I'm still in shock and I realise that,
I am dead but have been sent to Heaven,
I decide to explore beyond the depths of Heaven's gates.

Emma Harrison (16)
Cowley Language College

Through The Eyes Of A Burger

I lie in a grill
Helpless and weak
Waiting for someone
To come and eat my meat.

Garnished with salad, and ketchup too
A layer of cheese, just for you
I come with a bun, underneath and on top
I was bought from the corner shop.

Savour me
Enjoy me
Eat me while I'm hot
I was once a cow, but now I'm not!

Ryan Yates (13)
Cowley Language College

Untitled

Through the eyes of a dog
I sit in the corner and wait,
My owner wishes I would get lost in the fog,
But I never do.

I just wish,
I could go to another home,
They make me eat out of a dirty dish,
I might just run off to town.

I am a dog who is abandoned,
When the visitors come around
I always get through out the door,
But that is the only time I get out of the pound.

Once the visitors have gone,
My owner comes and takes me back to the pound.

Zoe Cook (13)
Cowley Language College

Through The Eyes of A Dog

I sit on the mud
And stare at the door
My owner comes out
And pushes me to the floor.

He looks really mad
And tries to grab me
But then I fight back
And bite his knee.

He screams in pain
But a neighbour sees
She comes running out
And says she'll help me.

She takes me inside
Then picks up the phone
She runs into the kitchen
And brings me a bone.

I live with her now
She adopted me
She takes me to the park
And sometimes the sea.

Gabby Longdon (13)
Cowley Language College

Through The Eyes Of . . . An Abandoned Baby

I cry and cry but no one hears,
And more and more I feel fear.

Why can't they hear me?
Where have they gone?
Do they not care about me, what have I done?

Mummy . . . Daddy . . . where have you gone?
I cry and cry but you don't come.
I feel so lonely,
I feel so sad,
How can you treat me like this Dad?

I cry and cry but you still don't come,
I might as well just give up,
I lie down and close my eyes,
Mum and Dad, I love you, goodbye.

Heather Davies (16)
Cowley Language College

Through The Eyes Of A Child

He hits me, he hurts me
He doesn't listen to my screams
He beats me and bruises me
And leaves me left in tears
How could he hurt me?
Why doesn't he care?
Daddy did I hurt you?
Please don't leave me in despair.

I crawl towards the open door, too tired for anymore,
Hopeless and helpless, I fall down to the floor.

My tears they fall and hit the floor
I'm getting very tired, the darkness now is hurting me like a hundred million knives.

I'm going now, I'll say goodbye,
Farewell my Dad, I'm sorry and goodbye . . .

Kathryn Leyland (16)
Cowley Language College

Through The Eyes of Someone Who Has Witnessed A Murder

Kicking and screaming, I woke with a fright
All I could remember was that terrible fight.
Kicking stamping, do as you please
Not even listening to his innocent pleas.

When it was all over, I ran over
I was unlucky because I fell over
'Help me! Help me! Listen to me plead
Please don't let this poor person bleed.'

I felt so helpless, I stood up to shout
'Why have you done this you lousy louts?'

When I got home I was freezing cold
Thinking how could people be so cruel and bold?
A life has gone. A life has been taken
All over a watch which was a cheap imitation.

Rhys Flynn (16)
Cowley Language College

In The Eyes Of A Bully

The blood, the blood
I hit and hit to impress my friends
But I don't like to do it
I do it to keep the friendship
The look that the victim gives me
Makes me feel hurt inside.
    I
    Wish
    I
    Could
    Stop
    It.

Simon Roughley
Cowley Language College

Untitled

My name is Lucy
I live with my dad
I love him so much
But I make him sad
Because every night
When we're alone
He hits me hard
But I never moan
No matter how much
I beg and plead
He hits me harder
And makes me bleed
He goes downstairs
I wipe my tears
The fridge door opens
That means more beers
I lie so still
Trying hard to sleep
Eyes wide open
With every creak
I often wonder
Why is life so bad?
And why do I make
My dad so sad?

Jamie Metcalfe
Cowley Language College

Through The Eyes Of A Dolphin

When I took my first breath of air
That's when I began to see her
My mum who had given me life.

From then we never parted
Not even when the season started
For the dreaded hunt for tuna.

Up until then my life was a joy
Up until we met that boy
The day I'll never forget.

There were a lot of hunters that day
So we chose a different way
To get to the place I call home.

That was a mistake
As a life they didn't give but take
The life was that of my mum.

I tried to help her to get free
But the net was hoisted out of the sea
Then I saw her die.

It was that boy I talked about
The one who was really tall and stout
But he didn't care.

When I saw her die
I began to cry
And still have bad memories to this day.

I can't stop crying
The thought of her dying
It's taken my soul away.

Yazmin Miah (14)
Cowley Language College

Through The Eyes Of A Dairylea Dunker

Dunk me, dunk me,
Stick me in your cheese.
Lick me, bite me,
Do as you please.

You can choose any flavour,
Original or spicy.
Do as you please,
Dunk me in your cheese.

I can be any shape,
Circle or square.
Dunk me in your cheese,
Or eat me bare.

Eat me, chew me,
Swallow me whole.
Dunk me in your cheese,
Or eat me out of a bowl.

Dunk me, dunk me,
Stick me in your cheese.
Lick me, bite me,
Do as you please.

Jacob Pettersen (13)
Cowley Language College

Through The Eyes Of A Rescue Dog

I sit in the corner until my owner gets home.
He punches and kicks me, he won't leave me alone.
He lies on the couch getting drunk from the beer,
The beer cans build up and so does my fear.

I bury my head in my rough hairy paws,
My owner charges at me, I can't stand those tough wars,
I stand unequipped with no weapons to fight,
My owner falls down and stays there through the night.

He wakes up next morning, he's in a bad way,
And there for my rescue is the RSPCA!
I get put in a cage, so helpless and stuck,
They give me food and water, a change in my luck.

I get homed in a building with other animals within,
They're so scrawny and ragged, some are so thin.
Days, weeks, months have passed and someone came for me at last!
They take me home and have me fed and put me in my cosy bed!

Rebecca Birchall (13)
Cowley Language College

Child Abuse

Punched in the head, beaten to the floor,
Getting my head rammed into the door.
He's broken my nose, he's broken my shoulder,
I've forgotten the day my father was sober.
My mother is dead, shot with a gun,
Since she has passed I've had no fun.
Why do I have a life of abuse?
I'd rather be an animal, maybe a moose.
I saw my father shoot her in the head,
It went through her brain, instantly dead.
He makes me sleep out in the dirt,
I pray one day I won't be hurt.
I've got a knife in my hand so when he returns,
I'll stab him in the heart and hope it burns.
He's just come in, I hope I succeed,
He's high on drugs, cocaine and weed.

Daniel Cheung (13)
Cowley Language College

Through A Dog's Eyes

Once I was a rescue dog feeling alone and scared,
Once I was frightened, hiding under stairs.
Now I am safe with someone who cares,
My new owner grooms me softly, brushing my fur.
Would any dog really want to be dirty and abused so bad?
Now I always wonder why my first owner was so mad.

When he walked in I would hide behind the chair,
So he couldn't find me and throw me down the stair.
I couldn't feel my leg, I could barely walk,
I just lay there when I heard him talk.
I always wondered what he was going to do next,
All I wanted to do was to get out of this mess.

I was just a little dog who needed some help.
I wanted to get away from this horrible hell.
Is it my fault that my owner was so cruel?
I always eat scraps, I'd rather eat gruel.

Now I am older, thought I had no life to live,
My new owners came and claimed me and had a lot of love to give.
My old life is over, my new one's just begun,
The darkness has ended and here comes the sun.

Jessica Graves (13)
Cowley Language College

Trigger!

I'm a baby panda, I've just been born,
I'm very cute and cuddly,
But my fur has already been torn!

My mum and dad are very big but I'm so much smaller,
Lying here all alone
Wishing I could be taller!

My mum hasn't given me a name
I am known as no one
And my brothers are the same!

Every day I'm getting bigger
My mum has chosen my name,
So say hello to baby Trigger!

Hayley Sharpe (13)
Croxteth Comprehensive School

Chair

I can be plastic
I can be wooden
So come and sit on me
But use a cushion.

I can be blue
I can be red
My legs can be metal
That's what I said.

People push me over
And throw me around
But people lose money
One or two pound.

I can be burnt
I can be broke
People sit on me
But then I choke.

Jake Riley (12)
Croxteth Comprehensive School

A Dog's Life

I was born in a kennel,
I never knew my mum,
I lived there for years
Abandoned by all.

I had lots of friends,
Scots and Swedes
But something was missing,
A family for me.

The day had come,
I was moving out,
To a small family,
In a very small house.

When I moved in,
I was loved and loved,
With a warm home,
And cuddly hugs.

Lauren Fox (12)
Croxteth Comprehensive School

Alex The Ant

I am a little ant
So very, very small
My name is Alex
I love to crawl.

I walk in long straight lines
Behind all my mates
We're ready to go out.
Hoping to get dates.

We all show off
To all the boys
And they made
Lots of noise.

One of them
Asked me out
But my mind
Was in doubt.

In the end
I said, 'Yes,'
But it was
A bad mess.

He made me
A small cake,
But that was
A mistake!

Alex Walker (12)
Croxteth Comprehensive School

A Small And Lonely Puppy

I am a small puppy,
But I have no name.
I was born in a kennel,
Which is where I remain!

My mum has been taken,
To a nice family I think.
My brothers and sisters,
Went faster than a wink!

I am still here,
Waiting for a family.
I hope someone comes soon
Because it's kind of lonely!

So here I am,
Still all alone,
No one will come,
I think no one wants me!

Sarah-Louise Rudkin (13)
Croxteth Comprehensive School

The Whip

I've seen a lot in my time,
But nothing is this bad,
A little boy's father
Makes me hit a boy named Chad.

It isn't fair, it isn't right,
It shouldn't happen now,
Every night before he sleeps,
Chad's dad makes him take a bow.

I'm only a little leather whip,
It's really not my fault,
Please don't hit the child anymore
Bring it to a halt.

I really don't like hitting Chad,
I think it's very cruel,
I wonder why his dad does it,
He is a great big fool.

Now that I am on my own
Inside this dark, smelly bin,
Will you, Lord, forgive me,
For every single sin?

Joseph Lea & John Pringle (12)
Croxteth Comprehensive School

The Kitten

I am a baby kitten
Who hasn't got a name
So pick me a name
If you are nice
Then I'd like to chase
After the mice
I sleep in the kitchen
On the floor
I always bang my head
On the kitchen door
When my mum
Says goodbye
I always break
Down and start to cry.

Madison Jones (12)
Croxteth Comprehensive School

The Sun

Early morning when you're asleep
I light up the skies and heat up the beach,
Now's the time you open your eyes,
Families are coming to the beach,
They sit on the sand
And paddle in the sea and eat ice cream.
As the afternoon starts and I'm at my hottest and highest
The beach is packed and the ice creams melted.
The volleyballs are being pelted,
The people are leaving,
It's time for tea, the sandy sandwiches aren't that nice.
I'm setting, ohhh,
How romantic, couples are kissing,
But there's something missing.
It's me!
I have set, now the job is the moon's while I have a snooze.

Ryan Bodell (13)
Croxteth Comprehensive School

The Whale!

I am a whale
I live in the sea
Why didn't they give
A name to me?

I am a sweet creature
My name is Phil
I have a big belly
As big as a hill.

I can be black
I can be blue
I would like to swim
The ocean through.

John Higham (13)
Croxteth Comprehensive School

Pencil

Sometimes I'm sharp
Sometimes I'm not
I can draw lines
I can draw dots.

When I am blunt
Sharpen me quick
Do not drop me
My lead is not thick.

Philip McGuinness (12)
Croxteth Comprehensive School

Doggy Airlines

I am a little puppy
I love to go on tours
So when I get my lead on
I run around on all fours.

I travel the world
Next I'm going to France
Then I am going to Brazil
To do my daily dance.

I love to chase cats
In and out of England
I also like chasing polar bears
All around Finland.

I like to dig holes
And to wag my tail
But when the farmer comes out
Then it's time to bail.

Sometimes I feel sad
When people chase me
Sometimes I think
Some people hate me.

Now it is time for dinner
I really love my food
Don't look at me while I eat
It is very rude.

Time to leave Brazil now
Got to go to Spain
Let's go to the airport
And board up on my plane.

Woof! Woof!

Luke Johnson (12)
Croxteth Comprehensive School

I'm In Love

I'm in love,
I feel like a dove.
Every time I look at him,
I become really dumb.

I'm not in love,
I just don't care.
Every time I walk past him,
I'll have my head in the air.

I'm in love.

Rebecca Johnson (11)
Croxteth Comprehensive School

Track Of Sand

Treading on this track of sand.
Sun high in this autumn sky.
Searching for a place to lie
On this track of sand.
Awaiting me a place of unknown beauty.
Hidden by ancient power flowing through a fallen tower.
Now my time is ending, it is time for someone to take my place.

John Brougham (11)
Croxteth Comprehensive School

Before Birth

Here I am swimming in my womb,
It's just like a cosy little room,
I spend all day happy and afloat,
Like a little sailor aboard a rocky boat,
Happy all day sucking on my thumb,
And as I came out I found what really was a mum,
But why is the so-called doctor smacking me on my bum?

Sam Westhead (11)
Croxteth Comprehensive School

No Master

Get me a mansion,
Yes Master.
Get me some furniture,
Yes Master.
Get me things for the kitchen,
Yes Master.
Get me things for the bathroom,
Yes Master.
Get me a bed.
Yes Master.
It looks nice doesn't it?
Yeah Master.
Pardon?
Yes Master.
Get me a smooth, yet rough, a chewy, yet hard
Jade-green jelly bean,
No Master!

Amanda O'Neill (11)
Croxteth Comprehensive School

Why?

Why is there a sky?
Why is there a moon?
Why is there a sun?
Will we find out soon?

Will I be a dancer?
Will I learn to sing?
Will I have good health?
What will my life bring?

How come we can't find out these things?
How come we don't know?
Can you say the day before
The way the wind will blow?

No one knows for certain
The day the Earth will end
No one knows for certain
And no one can depend!

Melissa Finnegan (12)
Croxteth Comprehensive School

You'll See

Read this poem and you will see
That I'm not the man I used to be.
I have changed in many ways
It must be a weird little phase.
If you hate me please forgive me
As my heart is very breakable.
My first sign of hate makes me drop to the floor
And soon I'll hate you even more.
Then I won't even look at you
Because you broke my heart torn in two pieces.
Torn apart!

Jack Kearns (12)
Croxteth Comprehensive School

Is There?

Is there a Heaven up in the sky?
Is there a mountain steep yet high?
Is there peace and not war?
I know there is rich and I know there is poor!

Is there a bond between father and son?
Is there a love between daughter and mum?
Is there a rose as red as can be?
Is there a love waiting for me?

What I want to know is there an answer
And will anyone ever cure cancer?
I hope this poem won't make you cry
But as we all know life goes by!

Natasha Todd (12)
Croxteth Comprehensive School

R We There Yet?

We're off to France today
We're goin' down the motorway
When the children say
'R we there yet?'
We go past the shop,
The children don't want to stop
And then they say
'R we there yet?'
We get on the ferry
The kids see their mate Terry
He gives them a berry
And then they say
'R we there yet?'
We get off the ferry
And say goodbye to Terry
We get in the car
We drive to a spa
And then I go to the bar
And then the children say
'R we there yet?'
We arrive at the hotel
We ring the bell
The doorman comes and lets us in
Then the children say
'R we there yet?'
Yes, we're there.

Joe Jackson (12)
Croxteth Comprehensive School

A Boy Called Pete

There was once a boy called Pete
Who had size fourteen feet.
His feet were like flippers
He couldn't get slippers
And on shoe sizes he's never been beat.

He goes to Crocky school
No one thinks he's cool.
He's in year eleven
Gets bullied by year seven
But he's very good in the pool.

Edward Abley (12)
Croxteth Comprehensive School

Winter Snowflakes

They fall from the sky,
Graceful and slow,
No one the same,
As far as we know.

Cold and silver,
Shiny like gold,
Forever it will last,
It's beauty and cold.

Lands in the snow
Its silver peeking out,
But where did it come from?
The north or south.

It finally melts,
Now it's in with the snow,
But is it still there,
Will we ever know?

Rachael McGowan (11)
Croxteth Comprehensive School

The Night

The moon hanging in the night
Its luminous glow so sly
When the full moon is out
Nobody wants to walk about.

The night's creatures running
From others, oh so cunning
The owls catching mice
With talons not very nice.

It's nature, the night is nature
It has its ways of being scary.

Natalia Ray (11)
Croxteth Comprehensive School

What's That Noise?

What's that noise?
I ask the boys
We all begin to wonder
Is that the thunder?
We are all in fear
As the thunder is near.

Liam Mullin (11)
Croxteth Comprehensive School

Childline

Alone. A word I ask myself,
Every morning, day and night.
Alone I say in the school toilets,
Myself, a scary sight.

Blue, black, purpley brown,
The colours I most relate to,
Your parents probably cook your tea,
Wash your clothes and love you.

So, who am I, reveal yourself you ask,
This story isn't just mine,
As my name is Tommy, I live without love
And once a week I will ring Childline.

Chelsea Nelson (12)
Holly Lodge Girls' College

The Man Who Never Spoke

There he was sitting in the gutter,
With everyone who passed, gave a loud stutter,
He begged day and night,
The coins he was spared, glistened in the moonlight.
He lived in the alley,
Where thugs claim they're scally.
He hid away till the morning sun,
So hungry and tired, he robbed a warm bun.
Again alone in the cold,
No one by his side, no one to hold,
No one to push him in the right direction,
Nobody to show him love and affection,
He roamed the streets day and night,
Looking for food with sure delight,
Living in poverty, he walked past shops and looked at pottery,
I bet he'd always wished he'd win the lottery,
Just to be known, just to be heard,
He lay on the grass and watched the birds,
He wanted to be known but he never spoke.
Nobody knew that night he took a stroke,
He lived in the cold, died when he was there,
By the stairs where he lived, the sign now says,
Beware!

Emma McCormick (13)
Holly Lodge Girls' College

School Time

I walk to school nearly every day
But sometimes it can be dark
As me and Georgia cut through Larkhill Park.
We get to the gate and hope we're not late,
Because sometimes our form teacher can be a bit of a nark.

I walk into my form room
Sir is about to mark us in
I sit down on my chair
Then I say, 'Yes Sir.'
We go to period one then two
Now it is break
I have tea, toast and cake.
Period three is on its way
I forgot my homework, what should I say?
Now it is lunch
I go on the hotside once again
My chips and sausage came to £1.10
Now period four and five have come
Then I go home and spend some time with my mum.

Patricia Fisher (12)
Holly Lodge Girls' College

The Unwanted

I am standing here in the cold,
They only threw me out because I'm old,
I am saying this to you, as I have no voice,
Of course it's not them humans, it's not their choice,
Humans aren't to blame,
It's not their fault I'm again in the rain,
I shall tell you how it all started,
Him and his new wife departed.

It is a Sunday in June,
The flowers in bloom,
The car arrives,
Then it starts to dive,
I run to the door to say goodbye,
I'm too late, he slams the door, and I sigh,
I can't help it if I cannot run,
It's because I am old, not because I am dumb!

Two weeks later they finally come back,
That's when he comes in and starts to attack,
She just starts to giggle and laugh,
I shut my eyes and everything goes black.

I wake up in the vets, people all around me,
My life just obviously isn't meant to be,
Then they say something about them,
I wish I could be back home in my little den,
Then I hear his voice in my head,
Everything goes black; am I dead?
I think I might be happy again, like when I was a puppy,
Even through all this I am proud to say my name was Lucky!

Charlotte Evans (12)
Holly Lodge Girls' College

A Dog Once Loved

I was just a small dog bought for Christmas Day,
I didn't know if my new family would like me
So all I could do was pray.
But my fears came true and I was abandoned one night,
Even though I thought this would happen,
It came as quite a fright.
All my hopes and dreams smashed,
My whole world had crashed.
I went from everything to nothing
All in one night,
I went from home to alleyway
Which is not a nice sight.
I beg for the scraps and I get all sorts,
The family abandoned me without giving me a thought.
I hate this new life of mine, it's awfully sad,
But not all humans are to blame, they're not all bad!
Even thought I'm old, scruffy and down on my luck,
I'm not afraid to speak out and yell my name which is Buck!

Jenny Oulton (13)
Holly Lodge Girls' College

My Cat Pennie

One day in the shining sun
I thought about my past
About the things I'd loved the most
And that included my cat.

He was big and black, his name was Pennie
I loved with all my heart
He was always there to cheer us up
We'd never be apart.

He would sleep on the couch and on the floor
But never on his bed
He always chased the neighbour's cat
I think he wanted him dead.

Mum and Dad would cuddle him
And squeeze him really tight
And late at night he'd fall asleep
And we'd say to him *'Goodnight.'*

Megan Price (12)
Holly Lodge Girls' College

Guinea Pigs

It's good being me
Hopping round all day
I love the feeling of being free
I just want to play
I hate all the cats
That hang around my cage
All the squeaking of the rats
I'm burning up with rage
Munching on my Weetabix
Eating all my veg
I hate the feeling of having ticks
Getting stuck between the hedge
I love a tickle on my belly
A pamper once in a while
After watching pepper-pig
I could run a mile.

Hannah Farrelly (11)
Holly Lodge Girls' College

Suspicious Cat

Suspicious cat
I love to get a little pat
Suspicious cat
I am a little bit fat
Suspicious cat
I like the scratching noises of a rat
Suspicious cat
I creep round at night looking for a fight
Suspicious cat
I like fish in my dish
Suspicious cat
That's what I am
A suspicious cat.

Demi McLoughlin (12)
Holly Lodge Girls' College

Pongo!

My owner's in work
I'm crying so loud
Surprise
The door bangs open
It's her, she's here
My friend is here
I ask for a stroke
I lie on my back
My tail wags excitedly
This feeling I love
The strokes and the pats
A brush and a groom
I'm upset, she's left the room
It's time for a nap
Upstairs on the mat
I lie while I sleep
And sleep I shall do.

Gaby Jones (12)
Holly Lodge Girls' College

Who Am I?

People fling me around,
They pull me around, up and down everywhere,
I get put in different places on a person's head,
I get people out of detention,
People twist me, break me, lose me,
I come in all different colours.
Ping! I hit the wall,
Nooooo! I'm down the side of a bed,
In the bottom of a person's make-up bag.
But now at least I have time to
Relax.

Lucy Hopkins (12)
Holly Lodge Girls' College

What Am I?

How would you feel if people were rough with you?
Think about it!
I'm in a room with no one else, I'm very lonely.
I get used nearly every day.
For the same thing, at the same time.
I get crushed and swung on!
I get scraped along the floor
And people hit me which makes me sore.
I get things graffitied on my back
And it hurts!
Which makes me sad!
I always have human legs wrapped around me!
I have chewing gum on by bottom!
People stand on me
And wipe their feet on me!
Would you like this to happen to you?
But on the other hand
I am always warm and I like meeting new people.
I feel hard and rough,
I don't have a smell,
But I can smell all different things,
But believe me, you don't want to know!
Can you guess what I am?
Shall I tell you?
I'm a chair!

Amanda McEwan (12)
Holly Lodge Girls' College

Untitled

I feel scared and frightened
I walk onto the stage
People are watching me
The microphone is in my face.
I stutter.
My heart pumping
Faster than a speeding car.
I start to sing
The scent of perfume
Hits my nose.
Singing louder
I dance around the stage.
People clap
I look about
I walk out the door
Millions of faces
Stare back
I walk off caring
In happiness.

Megan Jones (11)
Holly Lodge Girls' College

The Seasons

January turns its winter tale
February brings the rain and hail
March, white rabbit and spring is here
April, showers and summer's near
May, the swifts and swallows arrive
June, the roses come alive
July, the summer's in full swing
Warm summer days, August brings
September cools the warm summer breeze
October falls the autumn leaves
November days are dark and dim
December festive time begins.

Melissa Greaves (11)
Holly Lodge Girls' College

My Dog's Life

I am a dog that lays on the couch
Loved by my family
But also have doubts.
I hate my food but love my family's.
I go for walks, I see other dogs.
I don't like them, they don't like me.
They think I am a horrible breed.
They don't realise I have feelings too.
I hurt when people are cruel to me.
I'm loved a lot.
I know I am
When they go to school
I wait and wait for them to come home to me.

Laura Fraser (12)
Holly Lodge Girls' College

I Hate Being A Chair But Sometimes I Love Being A Chair

I hate being me
Getting swung on my two legs.
I hate being me
People sitting on me
Sticking chewy on my bottom.
I get drawn on
I get sticky.

Sometimes
I love being me.
When it's windy
I don't have to go outside.
Sometimes I get washed by the cleaners.

But sometimes
They hurt my feelings
By breaking my legs.

Demi Brooks (11)
Holly Lodge Girls' College

Blowing In The Wind

Blowing in the wind, it's pushing me around
My leaves being blown off my branches
Them being kicked, stood on, thrown at people
Keys, pens, even fingernails engraved into my insides
People pulling my arms and my legs
Apples being yanked out of my reach
I never get privacy
People, things, leaning on me, squashing me
Unable to breathe
Swings being made on me
The tight rope strangling around my neck
But then there's always the great help
I am helping the happy children hide behind me
Being the toilet for the dog from down the road
People having a romantic picnic under me
Blowing in the wind, it's pushing me around.

Beverley Paine (11)
Holly Lodge Girls' College

Everton FC

E very
V ery good
E nergy drink
R echarges you
T o give you the
O ption so that
N ow

F ootballers
C an work harder for their money!

Stephanie Murphy (13)
Holly Lodge Girls' College

Family

F riendship
A lways there for you
M um cooks the tea
I mportant to each other
L ike being near you
Y our friends for life.

Georgia Moss (12)
Holly Lodge Girls' College

Friends

Friends are kind
They don't really mind
All they want to do is hang around
People say we shall always stay
Best friends together
Always forever
That's what friends are for

They laugh
They joke
They cry
They sulk
But one thing, we are best friends
Together forever, always together.

Sarah Doyle (13)
Holly Lodge Girls' College

Beyonce

B rilliant
E njoyable
Y uppie
O pen-minded
N ever nervous
C arefree
E asy-going.

Keeley Wright (13)
Holly Lodge Girls' College

Homeless Person

As I lie there in the night,
Holding onto my bag tight,
I hear footsteps, it's a man with a knife,
I try to run away for my life
But it's too late, my belongings are gone
I don't have a penny left, not even one
My clothes are still wet from the night before,
I just lie there shivering on the floor.

Amy Currie
Holly Lodge Girls' College

Homelessness

Cold and alone when I am rejected
Foodless and thirsty when I am cramped
I beg all day and beg all night
Still not a penny to my name.

Hassled and injured when a drunk attacks me
Invisible and frozen because I just want money
Smelly and dirty because I haven't had a wash
The game I was in I have now lost.

Depressed and worried I may never find a home
Stomach cramps and illness make me moan
If I was rich I could buy a phone
To help me go and find a home.

Sleeping with headlice
It is really not nice
Nervous or relaxed or am I depressed?
Being homeless gets me very stressed.

Cold and alone when I am rejected
Foodless and thirsty when I am cramped.
I beg all day and beg all night
Still not a penny to my name.

Lauren Davies (14)
Holly Lodge Girls' College

Homelessness

H omeless like me get very lonely
O pportunities for me aren't very great
M oney means life just for me
E motions get the best of me
L ove is all I would wish for right now
E mpty doorways are my bedroom
S truggling I am, because of the way I live
S tarvation is hard for me to deal with
N ot much is a lot to me
E verything I need is just a dream
S kinny I am because of lack of food
S cared and frightened for knowing what's coming.

Katie Lewtas
Holly Lodge Girls' College

Homeless Makes You An Outsider

Why is it you do one thing wrong and from then on you are rejected
For the rest of your life?
Wet, cold and bruised all over, this is what it's like to live on the
Street on that concrete.
Nervous, worried, confused and scared,
This is what you feel when you are forced to do something you just
don't want to do.
But then in the world of homelessness you never have a choice,
Never have your say,
Kicked, punched, spat at and smacked.
To them my life is about being a punchbag.
Thirsty, hungry, so, so hungry and so ashamed,
Staring, pointing and belittling me, making me feel like an outsider.
No! I am an outsider, outside of the world of money, food and respect
Even though it's right there waiting for me
I can't have it ever! Because who would ever love me? After all I am a
nobody.
I'm not poor, I'm lower than poor.
I am lower than a rat, at least rats get food.

Kelsey Davies
Holly Lodge Girls' College

I Lie There

I lie there cold, scared and hungry
Anxious about what's going to happen next
Dark shadows walk into the night
Shivering on a rock-hard cold floor
Bruises appear on my skin
Today I got food from the bins
Wrapped up in old newspapers to keep me warm.

You feel so rejected
People walking straight past you looking as if you're dirt
When you beg for money
For food or drink or anything to stop this belly ache.

The worst is when it rains or even snows
No one comes out on the streets
But I still stand there hoping someone will walk past and give me
some money

Then I go to sleep again
Worrying if I'll make it to the next day
Then I wake up and do it all again.

Georgina Robinson (14)
Holly Lodge Girls' College

Homelessness

Sitting here on these cold floors again,
People stop and stare, but they don't really care.
They just keep walking by.
I feel so different to everyone else,
I just want to cry,
I am so bullied and victimised,
It makes me sigh.
The little shelter I get is on a cold floor, outside the shop door.
I feel so confused and lost.
Why did this happen to me,
Why did I lose my home and family?
People walk past and shout things to me,
They say, 'Why do you have to lie there and block the floor?'
Then I have to go and find a new shop door.
On Friday nights the public get worse,
They throw things and hit me and it really hurts.
I sometimes wish I could die,
It would be better than sitting here,
Living with fear,
Please just let me die.

Vanessa Rodick (13)
Holly Lodge Girls' College

Don't Be A Fool

A fate worse than death,
Put it to the test,
What do we get?
A chance for education,
Banged up inside these four walls,
Don't blame it on legalisation,
The only good cause, perfection.

Rubber pens, plastic chairs,
We've mastered the art of behaving,
Only see it as a chance of escaping,
The hell that we drink in,
The depression that we sink in,
Hopeful? Drowned.

Getting taught a way of learning,
Getting shot a way of yearning,
To! Be the big man, tough leader,
Be one of them up in court,
Life
Get dragged down - education?

Put them to the point,
Sit down, write down and succeed,
Be the long shot, drop the trigger,
Prison, jail, behind bars. It's a mug's game,
Education? Life's best lesson,
Bullet saved.

Katie Smith (16)
Holly Lodge Girls' College

Racism

All day long I sit around with nothing else to do
Life is hard with racism
It is for me not you.

To be a different colour is sometimes a horrible feeling
For all of the pain they've put me through
To them it's like I'm kneeling.

They think I'm not the same
Because of what I am
And here's me thinking that I'm their friend
When it was just a scam.

I wish I could fit in, the same colour and the same size
I'm fed up of their sickly jokes
And all of their racist lies.

Arizona-Lea Rice (13)
Holly Lodge Girls' College

Do They Know?

What is the meaning of life?
Is it really a question?
You could travel everywhere and never figure it out
There is no answer
There is just life
Do this, do that
We get told by the Government to work
The brainwashing that's done to us as a child
The gangs on every corner
Is the Government doing anything for them?
No! They're just letting them cause destruction
Attack anyone, do whatever you want
As long as you're not here
Their parents tell them
While they sit in drunk
There are a lot of things wrong in this world
But is the Government doing anything?
No! They just sit there every day
While someone is getting attacked
In their home
The kids are alone
Scared, all they can hear is shouting
Are we going to do something?
Or are we just going to sit while these children
Die in their homes?

Alexandra Watt (12)
Holly Lodge Girls' College

Waiting

Waiting in the dark,
Lonely and cold,
Waiting for him to come,
Waiting, waiting . . .

Hours later, still waiting,
Shivering in the dark,
Sneezing in the cold,
Hours later, still waiting . . .

Still alone in the dark,
Hopes to be collected soon,
Hobbles down on his four legs,
Still alone in the dark . . .

Days later, still there,
Still alone, still afraid,
Still waiting,
Days later, still there.

Few weeks later, still there,
Slowly starving to death,
Dog's eyelids slowly close,
Waiting for him to come.

Soraya Atherton (13)
Holly Lodge Girls' College

Toby And Me

Have you ever wondered what it's like to be a dog
Wandering around all alone,
Nobody understanding a word he says?
Well that's where my dog comes in.
My dog is different, my dog doesn't;
Sit around all day and chew my shoes (well sometimes he does)
My dog is actually my hero,
My dog stops me from feeling down,
He always cheers me up.
He should be wearing a crown,
He is a lovely dark tan, with some black and some brown,
He likes to play with toys, but never says 'hi' to boys,
He likes to make a bit of a noise when we listen to a CD or two,
But when we go to the park and the cows go moo,
My dog Toby says, *boo!*
He doesn't like pigeons, cats or mice,
Plus people who aren't very nice,
I love Toby with all my heart,
And will not stop until we part!

Jennifer Perrin (12)
Holly Lodge Girls' College

When I Become Homeless

I became homeless at sixteen,
Now I'm not a beauty queen,
Leaving behind my family
Was the hardest thing,
Every day I wonder how life would have been.
I'm hungry, thirsty, tired and scared,
Still I feel like no one cares.
Sitting on the streets I am cold,
Choose your place wisely I have been told.
Drunken men, drunken girls
Often try and steal what's left of my pearls.
When they're gone I'll have nothing left,
No memories of my family
Due to theft.
What will be left of me?

Ashleigh Coleman (13)
Holly Lodge Girls' College

Walking To His Own Beat

In the deep, dark depths of the street stands a social outcast
Who walks to his own beat.
Oblivious to me and you
He stands there depressed, unable to move.
Rejected from society, nervous and alone,
Uncomfortable, sad, anxious, missing a home.
Hungry, restless, unable to sleep,
Makes no sound, not even a peep.
Sleeping in bus shelters, derelict and cold,
Longing and hoping for someone to hold.
Damp and dirty with bruises on his skin
In a fight to keep warm, he steals newspapers from bins.
A sad old dosser who stands outside shops,
Begging, asking, pleading for jobs.
Then he is alone in the street
Walking on to his own beat.

Laura Jones
Holly Lodge Girls' College

Blown Over By The Wind!

Trees, trees sway in the breeze,
The wind is bad which makes me sad,
There is a tree next to me that looks as if it's about to be,
Blown over by the wind!

I think I had better run because,
Soon it will come tumbling from the sky,
All that way up high! It is going to be,
Blown over by the wind!

I'm at the end of the road,
I can see the load,
Tumbling from the sky, all that way up high,
It has been . . .
Blown over by the wind!

Laura Davidson (11)
Liverpool College

Flowers . . .

Flowers are delicate,
Flowers are rare,
Giving someone a flower,
Really shows that you care.

Roses are red,
Violets are blue,
Some flowers are covered,
In pollen - achoo!

Even in summer,
When they make you sneeze,
Flowers still look beautiful,
Blowing in the breeze.

Irises are purple,
Lilies are white,
They stain your carpet,
But that's alright!

Daisies look pretty,
In the golden sun,
Flowers are lovely,
Flowers are fun!

Asha Ray (12)
Liverpool College

Life

Just sat here thinking about life,
Wondering which things I have done right.
Now realisin' these tingz overcome the bad,
Which I am happy about and I am glad
Yo, it's because of all da wrongs that I'm writing these songs,
Because of the rights that I can finally see da light.
One ting I've learnt in life is you don't get many tru' friends,
Someone that you and she can borrow and lend,
Someone you can rely on to be there,
Who you know truthfully really does care,
These people are hard to come across,
You may think you have someone
Then they turn away and you're left feelin' lost.
What about love and hate?
Are these feelings we should respect or hate?
See love can turn to hate,
Suppose you can either end up feeling sad or great.
Whatever choice you make you're gonna pay.
Now what I'm gonna say,
Is no matter how old you are you learn something new each day,
Go on, take these words in, maybe look at them as advice.
They may come in useful at some point in your life.

Naomi Llewllyn (16)
Redbank Community Home

Teddy's Poem

Life's like an empty hole
No one to turn to
No one to look up to
I turned to drugs; turned to crime
I even left my family behind,
But now it's too late
Too late to turn back time
But now I'll change
Leave here with my head held high.

Sherrie Tedstone (15)
Redbank Community Home

The Girl I Knew

(In memory of Yasmin)

The girl I knew was so gentle and kind
You asked her for help and she just didn't mind.

Whenever, wherever you saw her, she had a smile on her face
She just stood there with her beauty and grace.

The happy times we used to share
Prancing around like we just didn't care
Pillow fights, dress-up games
Calling each other silly names.

She had a strong heart that no one could break
Disagreements we had was a huge mistake
I think of her now with tears in my eyes
The feeling of loss you just can't disguise . . .

Ashleigh Marr (13)
St Augustine of Canterbury Catholic High School, St Helens

Roads

Roads go ever on and on,
Under star and under tree.

Roads go ever on and on,
Past the beaches and the sea.

Roads go ever on and on,
Through the merry flowers of June.

Roads go ever on and on,
By the grass and the steep sand dune.

Roads go ever on and on,
Over the mountains and hills so steep.

Roads go ever on and on,
Near the happily roaming sheep.

Roads go ever on and on,
Stretching past the grass overgrown.

Roads go ever on and on,
To the meadows they long have known.

Robert Hurst (13)
St Augustine of Canterbury Catholic High School, St Helens

Flag And Flame

It's not a sport; it's not a game,
Fighting for their flag and flame!
A mission for all to fulfil,
One thing on their mind, to kill.

Led into the vulture's lair,
What has been, war declared?
Fighting for their lives in sorrow,
Wonders if they'll live tomorrow,
Fighting, killing, all in vain,
In the sleet, the snow, the rain,
One stray bullet, one stray shot,
Now they're dead, but never forgot.

'Line their lungs with lead' they say,
People, monks and priests do pray,
Humanity's weakness, glory and fame,
Fighting for their flag and flame!
All mankind live to die,
Not in war, their helpless cry.

Daniel Roberts (12)
St Augustine of Canterbury Catholic High School, St Helens

Friends Are Forever

Of all life's riches nothing could be
More precious than the friends that belong in me
The ones we confide in, the ones we trust
Depend on, rely on, that's a must
Memories we've shared will last in my mind
The good, the great, whatever kind
We've got a friendship nobody can break
We've got the greatest kind of love God's ever made
I think you're so fabulous I have to say
We'll be best friends till our very last day
You are always there for me, just like friends do
And I am proud to say my best friend is you!

Chelsea Barker (13)
St Augustine of Canterbury Catholic High School, St Helens

Susie And The War

Bombs dropping everywhere,
I don't understand how some people just don't care,
Out to the shelter we all run,
We sit in the darkness and have no fun,
We hear the sirens and go back inside,
I get sick of running and trying to hide.
I share my room with my sister and her mouse,
And on the next bomb scare, that's where I stayed,
Inside my little house.
I sit there in darkness, when I hear the bomb drop outside,
My name is Susie, and you have just read the story of how I died.

Nicola Clarke (13)
St Augustine of Canterbury Catholic High School, St Helens

Words Of Hope

The world gives up on you,
Unfortunately this is nothing new.
You are great, as good as can be,
But people do not see.
They mess you up and get you down,
They give you that discouraging frown.
You feel so alone,
Wanted by none.
So at night you sit and you cry,
During the day you stare at the sky.
Writing these poems all day long,
As you listen to the words of your song.
You keep yourself going through
The pain, which is not so new.
But that is life, it happens to the best,
People break your heart; all you can do is rest
Wait for someone to care for you and fix it,
Or your life ends with a little quick slit.
But do not ever go down that road,
I've been there, it isn't good, but as that princess kisses a toad
There is hope for everyone, you just need to persevere,
One day someone will care for you and hold you so dear.

Lee Gavin (15)
St Augustine of Canterbury Catholic High School, St Helens

Alone

When you're alone,
There's no one beside you.
No one you can trust
And no one you can talk to.

When you're alone,
You wish you were dead.
You even cry at night,
Tucked up in bed.

When you're alone,
You feel that no one's on your side.
You feel like you're wasting everyone's time,
There's no one in which you can confide.

That's how I feel
I feel so alone
No one listens to me
I'm all on my own.

Melissa Mower (14)
St Augustine of Canterbury Catholic High School, St Helens

School Mornings

The alarm kept buzzing down my ear
As I clambered out of bed
Getting dressed for school
And getting the bike out the shed
I felt like going back to bed
Racing down to school
Before the bell goes off
Ring, ring, ring
The bell went off as I locked
My bike up
The teacher
Going on at me
Where have you been?
I walked to my chair
The teacher was getting the register out
And called my name
First I didn't answer
And she shouted at me
That made me jump and I shouted, 'Yes
Mrs'
She sent me to the Head
I walked into the headmaster's office
I could feel my eyes drop,
And then she said to me,
'What do you want?'
I overslept and I'm too tired
She rang my mum up
She came and picked me up
I felt like the luckiest boy on Earth
When I was jumping back into bed
Then I remembered all the poor souls
That had to stay in school.

Liam Seddon (11)
St Augustine of Canterbury Catholic High School, St Helens

Magic Minute

The pulsing of the music, the constant beat,
Makes me want to move my feet
Make-up, costumes and the crowd's loud cheer
Round by round the final draws near.

The solo performance, all eyes are on you,
Smile at the judges, throw a wink in or two,
Dancing real hard, just wanting to win it,
Weeks of hard work for that one magic minute.

The dancing is tough but the waiting is tougher,
The longing to win makes the nerves really suffer,
They call out my number, I stutter and stammer
Because he announces the winner is Hannah.

Hannah Barr (11)
St Augustine of Canterbury Catholic High School, St Helens

Young Writers Information

We hope you have enjoyed reading this book - and that you will continue to enjoy it in the coming years.

If you like reading and writing poetry drop us a line, or give us a call, and we'll send you a free information pack.

Alternatively if you would like to order further copies of this book or any of our other titles, then please give us a call or log onto our website at www.youngwriters.co.uk

Young Writers Information
Remus House
Coltsfoot Drive
Peterborough
PE2 9JX

(01733) 890066